BLIND ALLEY

by Jack Popplewell

SAMUEL FRENCH

FOR AMATEUR PRODUCTION ENQUIRIES

UNITED KINGDOM AND WORLD
EXCLUDING NORTH AMERICA
licensing@concordtheatricals.co.uk
020-7054-7200

Each title is subject to availability from Concord Theatricals,
depending upon country of performance.

USE OF COPYRIGHTED MUSIC

USE OF COPYRIGHTED THIRD-PARTY MATERIALS

IMPORTANT BILLING AND CREDIT REQUIREMENTS

CHARACTERS

(in the order of their appearance)

JOHNNY FARRELL ⎫
DAVE FARRELL   ⎬ brothers
MIKE FARRELL   ⎭

"CALICO"

MRS FINNEGAN

PATRICK RYAN

AN OLD MAN

SYNOPSIS OF SCENES

The action of the Play passes in the living-room of the Farrells' lodgings in a midland city

ACT I

SCENE 1   A spring evening

SCENE 2   An evening, three weeks later

ACT II

Morning, a fortnight later

ACT III.

SCENE 1   Morning, three days later

SCENE 2   Morning, three days later

Time—the present

BLIND ALLEY

ACT I

Scene—*The living-room of the Farrells' lodgings in a midland city. A spring evening.*

There are windows LC and RC of the back wall showing the dingy roofs of the dingy city. A door down R leads to the landing and main entrance, and a door up R leads to a bedroom. The fireplace is L and there is a sink in the corner up L. There are various articles of inexpensive furniture. A divan RC; a sideboard R; a table and three chairs LC; easy chairs above and below the fireplace; a small chair down R and a gramophone up R. The room is lit by an electric pendant C.

(See the Ground Plan at the end of the Play)

When the CURTAIN *rises, the window curtains are open but the light is on and a fire burns in the grate. A violin can be heard off, the melody is "If I Should Fall in Love Again".* DAVE FARRELL *is seated above the table, finishing his supper of bread, cheese and tea. He is a slight, nervous youth, aged nineteen. He is a clerk in the offices of Mallaby's Iron Foundry. His clothes are neat, clerkly and inconspicuous.* JOHNNY FARRELL, *Dave's elder brother, is standing by the window up* RC, *gazing out. He is tall, attractive and well-dressed. He has a city air about him, in marked contrast to Dave and the eldest brother Mike.* JOHNNY *is slick, intelligent, but at the moment, unsuccessful.*

JOHNNY (*turning and moving* LC) You've got a wonderful place here, Dave. H. and C., all mod. cons., and Kreisler to give recitals underneath your window (*He moves down* L)
DAVE (*smiling*) He's about a hundred years old.
JOHNNY. And still learning.
DAVE. He only knows one tune.
JOHNNY (*moving up* C) Doesn't he get tired of hearing it? (*He moves up* RC)
DAVE. Maybe he doesn't listen. He stands at the corner of the street. He's harmless.

· (*The violin music gradually diminishes in volume until it is no longer audible*)

JOHNNY. A beggar and his fiddle, eh? What a life!
DAVE. Are you sure you won't have anything to eat?

JOHNNY (*looking through the window up* RC; *abstracted*) I had a meal before I came up here.

DAVE. It's lousy cheese, but the tea's all right.

JOHNNY. The place hasn't changed, Dave. Same old skyline.

DAVE. Beautiful, isn't it?

JOHNNY. I always hated it.

DAVE. So do I.

JOHNNY. It is an industrial city with a population of four hundred thousand. A centre of the automobile industry. Lovers of antiquity will find interest in an old abbey knocked over by Oliver Cromwell in ten-sixty-six.

DAVE (*smiling*) What're you reading from?

JOHNNY. The Town Hall is a splendid example of advanced construction which created enormous discussion when formally opened in seventeen-eighty-three by William the Conqueror.

DAVE. Is that in the guide book?

JOHNNY. What a dump. (*He moves down* C)

DAVE. Not like London, eh, Johnny? Why have you come back?

JOHNNY (*crossing down* L) I had to. It's my spiritual home.

DAVE. How?'

JOHNNY (*moving to the fireplace*) It's a second-rate town. I'm a second-rater. So we belong together.

DAVE. I thought you were getting along fine.

JOHNNY. I was.

DAVE. What happened?

JOHNNY. Oh, a long run of losers. I lost five hundred at Ascot. Three at Lincoln. A packet at Windsor. I hadn't enough wool on my back to stand it.

DAVE. Oh.

JOHNNY (*moving to the chair* L *of the table*) If I hadn't left quietly, I'd have had a civic send-off. I owe every bookie in town. They're after my blood. (*He turns the chair and sits astride it, the wrong way round, resting his arms on the back*) What about you and Mike? How's things?

DAVE. Oh—routine. Nothing ever happens. You know.

JOHNNY. What do you do?

DAVE. We're at Mallaby's.

JOHNNY. Mallaby's Foundry?

DAVE. Yes.

JOHNNY. Employ a lot of men, don't they?

DAVE. Couple of thousand.

JOHNNY. You're in the office?

DAVE (*nodding agreeably*) It isn't exciting.

JOHNNY. What's Mike do?

DAVE. He's in the Yard. It's heavy work, but he's well paid.

JOHNNY. He'll be foreman, eh?

DAVE. He *was*. If things don't suit him he flies off the handle That doesn't make him popular.

JOHNNY. Throws his weight about, you mean?

DAVE. Nobody'll work under him.

JOHNNY. So he's back in the ranks. Mike always had a grievance against the world. Now he'll have another.

DAVE. Mr D'Arcy's looked after him.

JOHNNY (*enthusiastically*) Old D'Arcy!

DAVE. He knew Mike when he was a baby. He's the only one who can handle him. When they give Mike his cards Mr D'Arcy puts in a word for him and then kids him into staying on. Mike thinks he's doing *him* a favour.

JOHNNY (*smiling*) Poor Mike! Poor, dumb, quarrelsome, misunderstood Mike.

(DAVE *rises, picks up his cup and saucer, goes to the sink and rinses them*)

DAVE. There's one bit of news that'll knock you over.

JOHNNY. What?

DAVE. He's going to be married.

JOHNNY (*alarmed*) Who?

DAVE. Mike.

JOHNNY. No!

DAVE (*wiping the cup and saucer*) Yes, sir. He's going to be married.

JOHNNY (*laughing*) He never had a girl in his life.

DAVE (*crossing with the cup and saucer to the sideboard*) He's got one now. (*He puts the cup and saucer in the sideboard cupboard*)

JOHNNY (*rising*) Well, well, well! (*He turns the chair*)

DAVE (*turning from the sideboard*) I'm glad you're back, Johnny, because I'm worried about it. Perhaps you can do something.

JOHNNY (*crossing to the divan; puzzled*) What about? (*He takes a newspaper from his overcoat pocket*)

DAVE (*moving to R of the divan*) About Mike and—and this girl.

JOHNNY. Who? Me?

DAVE. Yes, Johnny.

JOHNNY (*facing Dave*) You mean interfere?

DAVE (*nodding*) She's no good, Johnny. She's no good at all.

JOHNNY (*putting the paper on the divan*) What can *I* do? (*He picks up his overcoat and hat from the divan*)

DAVE (*awkwardly*) You might talk him out of it.

JOHNNY (*moving up C and hanging his coat and hat on the hooks*) I might talk myself into a thick ear.

DAVE (*following Johnny up C*) He'd listen to you. He always did.

JOHNNY (*turning to face Dave*) What's wrong with her?

DAVE (*crossing to the fireplace; embarrassed*) I don't know. It's—something about her. She's . . . Johnny, I can't describe it. Just something. (*Hastily*) He spends all his money on her.

JOHNNY. He's twenty-one, Dave. (*He moves above the table*) In fact he's thirty-one. You're nineteen. He's supposed to know his own mind.

DAVE. I knew more about women when I was thirteen than
he'll ever know. He's a dope. She's making a fool out of him.
Somebody ought to do something. (*He sits in the easy chair down* L)
JOHNNY. What's she look like?
DAVE. You'll see—she'll be along. He's crazy about her.
JOHNNY (*moving down* LC) Pretty?
DAVE. She's all right to look at.
JOHNNY. I can't imagine old Mike with a girl. Not a pretty one.
(*He crosses down* R) Some old cow, maybe, but not an attractive
one. What's her name.
DAVE. Calico.
JOHNNY. Calico? That isn't a name.
DAVE. She comes from Liverpool. Her grandfather was a
Spaniard, or a Mexican or something. It's Gallegos, really, but it
isn't easy to say. What they called her sounded like Calico and it
stuck.
JOHNNY (*moving* C) What's she doing in this back-of-the-woods
town?
DAVE. Hell, I don't know, Johnny. Wait till you see her. She
was a chorus girl—or something—and came here in a dud show—
got stranded.
JOHNNY. And settled here?
DAVE. Something like that. Her real name's Helen.
JOHNNY (*moving to the divan and lying on it*) Well, look, Dave, if
Mike wants to marry her it's his own affair. Not yours. Not mine.
I'll give you some advice. Never interfere between a woman and
her baby, and a man and his girl. You get no medals for it. And
you might get a broken neck. (*He looks at his newspaper*)
DAVE. Wait till you see her.
JOHNNY. I'm waiting.
DAVE (*rising and moving up* C) Anyhow, I'm glad you're back.
What're you going to do?
JOHNNY. I haven't decided.
DAVE. I could speak to Mr D'Arcy.
JOHNNY. What about?
DAVE. A job for you. With us.
JOHNNY. At Mallaby's?
DAVE. Why not?
JOHNNY (*lowering his paper*) Yes. (*He pauses. Thoughtfully*) That's
nice of you, Dave. But I have a couple of quid left. When I take
a job I want to be sure it's the right one. I'll take a look around,
first. See what I mean? (*He returns to his paper*)

(*Footsteps and voices are heard off* R)

MRS FINNEGAN (*off*) No consideration for my rheumatism.
Doors open all over the house.
MIKE (*off*) Did I leave the door open, Mrs Finnegan? That's
twice in one day—it's lucky.

Dave (*crossing to the door down* R) Sounds like Mike. (*He opens the door*)

(Mike Farrell *enters down* R. *He is an exceptionally big and powerful man, aged thirty-one. He carries his coat and wears a hat which he does not remove. He crosses to* LC *and puts his coat on the chair* L *of the table*)

(*He closes the door*) Johnny's back.

Johnny (*rising and moving* C) How're you, Mike, you big elephant?

Mike (*moving to* L *of Johnny and hugging him*) We-l-l! (*He smiles broadly*) All dressed up, he is. Ruddy capitalist. So you've come slumming, eh?

Johnny. That's right, Mike (*He puts his paper on the table*)

Mike. One half of the world doesn't know how the other half lives, eh?

Johnny. They do their best to find out.

Mike (*shaking Johnny by the hand*) Well, it's good to see you. What brings you back? Police after you?

Johnny. Not yet.

Mike (*circling Johnny*) You look prosperous. Yes, sir, you've done well for yourself.

Johnny. I'm broke.

Mike. No?

Johnny. Very broke.

(Mike, *chuckling with amusement, sits* R *of the table and helps himself to bread and cheese*)

Mike. You haven't changed a bit.

Johnny. Neither have you. You still behave like a drunken Irishman. (*To Dave*) Does he go to bed wearing his hat?

Mike (*grinning*) I catch cold without it.

Johnny (*crossing to* LC) Doesn't he even take it off for his girl, Dave? (*To Mike*) They tell me you got yourself a girl, Mike.

Mike. That's so, Johnny.

Johnny. Where is she?

Mike. She's coming. She's gone up to her room first.

Johnny. She lives here?

Dave (*crossing to the easy chair down* L) Upstairs. That's how we met her. (*He sits*)

Johnny. I see. Well, I want to meet her, too.

Mike. She's coming. (*He rises and moves to the sideboard. To Dave*) Why isn't there any beer poured out? We've got a guest. Where's your manners?

Dave. He wouldn't have any beer.

Mike. He will now.

Dave. We haven't any.

Mike. Well, fetch some. (*He moves down* R)

DAVE. With what? I'm broke. This is Wednesday—not Friday.

JOHNNY (*moving* C) Look, boys, this is on me.

MIKE (*moving* RC) It isn't, you know. (*He fumbles in his pocket. To Dave*) How much have you got?

DAVE. Two and fourpence ha'penny. And I need my bus fare in the morning.

MIKE (*to Johnny*) He's a mean little skinflint. You wouldn't believe it.

DAVE (*to Johnny*) I earn six-ten a week. He can make nine. If he didn't throw it all away on *her* he wouldn't have to sponge on me.

MIKE (*crossing to Dave; angrily*) Why you little . . .

JOHNNY (*smiling placatingly*) Break it up there. Remember Ma's motto on the wall. "Let Brotherly Love Continue." I said it's on me. (*He takes a note from his pocket*)

MIKE (*to Dave*) One of these days I'm going to put you across my knee and smack the daylight out of you.

DAVE (*rising*) He's always broke. She gets every penny.

JOHNNY (*crossing quickly to Dave*) Here, take this. (*He gives the note to Dave*) Go wherever you do go and get some beer. It's my treat.

DAVE (*crossing to* C) It's just round the corner.

JOHNNY (*pushing Dave down* R) That's fine. Run along, Dave.

(DAVE *exits down* R. MIKE *crosses to the sideboard, picks up a packet of cigarettes and offers them to Johnny.* JOHNNY *strikes a match and they both light up*)

When are you planning to get married, Mike? Soon?

MIKE (*slowly*) We've no plans. (*He crosses, picks up his coat and hangs it on the hooks*)

JOHNNY (*moving to the table*) Can you afford it. (*He sits* R *of the table and picks up his newspaper*)

MIKE (*crossing to the fireplace*) No. (*Quickly*) But I will.

JOHNNY. You'll need plenty.

MIKE. I'll get it. How long are you back for, Johnny?

JOHNNY. I don't know.

MIKE. You say you're broke?

JOHNNY. Flat. I owe a thousand pounds or more.

MIKE (*whistling incredulously*) Whew! You had a good time, didn't you? Women?

JOHNNY. Fast women and slow horses.

MIKE. Yes. You always were the gambler.

JOHNNY. Mike, is it true you're spending everything on your girl? I mean—everything.

MIKE (*turning and kneeling at the fire*) It's my own money. (*He pokes the fire*)

JOHNNY. I'm not lecturing. I'm asking.

MIKE. I don't like to be mean. You know me.

JOHNNY. If she's keen to be married she won't want you to throw it away.

MIKE. She's young, Johnny. She's just a kid.

JOHNNY (*rising and moving* C) What d'you buy? Furniture?

(MIKE *is silent*)

(*He moves up* C) I guess it isn't my business. I'm sorry.

MIKE. Johnny, she's pretty. I like to give her a good time. (*He rises and turns*) If I don't there's plenty who will.

JOHNNY (*moving down* C) Are you in love with her?

MIKE (*embarrassed*) She's so—so small, Johnny. I could break her in two so easy. Sometimes I'm afraid I will. And she's pretty. They call her Calico.

JOHNNY. It's a funny name.

MIKE. Yes. But it's cute. I like it.

JOHNNY (*crossing and sitting in the easy chair down* L) You're in love all right.

MIKE (*laughing*) I'm thirty-one. It's time, eh?

JOHNNY. I suppose so.

MIKE (*sitting in the easy chair* LC) She's been an actress. I never met an actress before. She works at a dance hall.

JOHNNY. Doing what?

MIKE. Dancing. She's a professional.

JOHNNY. You don't dance.

MIKE. No. I'm like a fish out of water. You can dance with her, Johnny. You were always keen, weren't you?

JOHNNY. Sometimes.

(*There is a knock at the door down* R)

Who's that?

(MIKE, *beaming, rises, crosses to the door down* R *and opens it.*
CALICO *enters down* R. *She is slender and very attractive indeed. She wears a sweater and trousers. Her manner, contrary to the impression created of her, is not hard or tough. It is more apparently ingenuous. She crosses to* RC. MIKE *closes the door, moves to* CALICO, *stands beside her and they both look at* JOHNNY, *who rises.* MIKE *grins but cannot find words*)

Well, come on. Introduce me to the lady.

MIKE (*holding Calico's hand*) This is my girl, Johnny. (*To Calico*) He's my brother. I told you about him.

JOHNNY. Hello, Calico.

CALICO. Hello—Johnny.

MIKE (*to Calico*) He's been living in London. Johnny's the smart one of the family.

JOHNNY. But I'm broke. So you really are called Calico?

CALICO (*moving* C) It's just a nickname.

MIKE. Calico—it's a piece of material.

JOHNNY. I'll say it is. Funny thing about women in men's jerseys. It makes 'em look more like women than ever.

MIKE (*shyly*) Look, I'll go after Dave. He can't carry a dozen bottles. You two get to know each other, eh?

JOHNNY. Don't be long. We're thirsty.

(MIKE *exits awkwardly down* R)

(*He takes a packet of cigarettes from his pocket and moves to* L *of Calico*) Cigarette? (*He proffers the packet*)

CALICO (*taking a cigarette*) So you're Johnny?

JOHNNY. That's right.

CALICO. I've heard a lot about you.

JOHNNY. You beat me there. You came as a surprise.

CALICO. Why?

JOHNNY (*lighting her cigarette*) Mike never ran after girls.

CALICO. He has a lot to learn.

JOHNNY. Are you teaching him?

(CALICO *smiles*)

We're going to be relations, I'm told. You and I.

CALICO (*crossing below Johnny to the fireplace*) Are we?

JOHNNY. So they tell me.

CALICO. Do you approve?

JOHNNY. I don't know you.

CALICO. I'm easy to get to know. No frills. No tricks.

JOHNNY. Then you're not as feminine as you look.

(*There is a silence.* JOHNNY *thoughtfully surveys Calico*)

CALICO. What are you staring at me for?

JOHNNY. Just wondering.

CALICO. Wondering what?

JOHNNY. You know, Ma brought us three boys up. She was no bigger than you, and we were scared stiff of her. We loved her, too. She thought we were wonderful.

CALICO. She couldn't be mistaken.

JOHNNY (*sitting on the right arm of the easy chair* LC) Ma always thought I was the responsible one. Dave was nervy, liable to brainstorms: Mike, big and strong, but easily led. She reckoned Mike would get himself into trouble if she wasn't there to look after him.

CALICO. What are you getting at?

JOHNNY. I just want you to know Mike's background. Ma died a couple of years ago. Mike's older than I am but she made me promise I'd keep an eye on him. Help him. You know . . .

CALICO. You being the smart one.

JOHNNY. That's about it. You see . . .

CALICO. Why don't you say what's on your mind? I'm a simple

person, Johnny. I don't understand if I don't get it straight. Come on now. Let's have it.

JOHNNY. There's nothing on my mind, Calico. It's just—play the game with Mike, will you?

CALICO. Why shouldn't I?

JOHNNY. You know how it is—some girls are mercenary.

CALICO (*crossing to* C) So they tell me. So are some men. All men. For crying out loud, he's big enough to take care of himself, isn't he? Suppose I tell him what you said. What'll he think about it?

JOHNNY. He wouldn't think. His brain's practically unused.

CALICO (*sitting* L *of the table*) He'd pin your ears back. (*She smiles*) And you're kinda pretty. I wouldn't want him to hurt that profile. What have you got against me, anyway?

JOHNNY. Nothing. He's crazy about you. I only mean—if you're indifferent—don't take him too far along the road.

CALICO. He's a nice boy. He's got muscles like an all-in wrestler. And a heart as soft as butter. (*She fingers her scarf*) He bought me this.

(JOHNNY *ignores the scarf, rises, moves to Calico, takes her left wrist and gently raises it. A platinum and diamond wrist-watch can be seen*)

JOHNNY. This is nice. But *really* nice.

CALICO. I like it.

JOHNNY. I'll bet. (*He releases her wrist and moves up* R) Did Mike give it to you?

CALICO. What do *you* think?

JOHNNY. I hope he didn't.

CALICO. Why?

JOHNNY. Because I know something about those things. (*He moves down* R) I bought a girl a watch like that last year. I'd won a hell of a lot of money on the Derby.

CALICO. So what?

JOHNNY (*leaning on the down right corner of the table*) So Mike couldn't afford to buy it unless he held somebody up for the money.

CALICO (*thoughtfully surveying her watch*) Is it very good?

JOHNNY. Don't you know?

CALICO. I thought—maybe—thirty pounds.

JOHNNY (*laughing*) A hundred and thirty more like.

CALICO. You're kidding.

JOHNNY. Where did you get it?

CALICO (*evasively*) A friend. You sure about what you said?

JOHNNY. Of course I am. Close on two hundred. Those are diamonds. And platinum isn't picked up in the streets. (*He moves* C) Mike didn't give it to you, did he?

CALICO. I said not. A friend.

JOHNNY. You've got nice friends.

CALICO. Yes, I have.

JOHNNY (*crossing to* LC) Lucky you!

CALICO (*rising*) Why don't you like me, Johnny?

JOHNNY. Who says I don't?

CALICO (*moving to* R *of him*) Talking about your mother. She wouldn't approve of me, would she?

JOHNNY. That's no criticism. Mothers only approve of the stay-at-home type. Then they're ready to hand over.

CALICO. But not to such as me.

JOHNNY. The peak of a mother's career is when the right person plucks the apple of her eye. (*He crosses to the fireplace*) You may be right, I don't know.

(DAVE *and* MIKE *enter down* R. *Each carries six bottles of beer which they put on the table.* CALICO *goes to the sideboard, picks up a tray, takes four glasses from the sideboard cupboard and puts them on the table.* MIKE *gets a bottle opener from the sideboard, opens the bottles and* DAVE *fills three glasses*)

MIKE. This is the stuff to give 'em.

CALICO. We thought you'd got lost.

MIKE. If I hadn't gone after him he'd have broken half of 'em.

DAVE (L *of the table*) I'm not a juggler. What's Calico drinking?

MIKE (*above the table*) She's drinking beer.

DAVE. How d'you know she is?

MIKE. 'Cos we've nothing else. It'll make her grow.

DAVE (*to Calico*) There's a bottle of sherry in my room. Wouldn't you rather . . . ?

MIKE. Sherry! Listen to him.

CALICO (*moving to* R *of the table*) I'll have beer. (*She pours a glass of beer for herself*)

MIKE. Good girl. (*To Dave*) I didn't know you'd a bottle of sherry.

DAVE. There's plenty you don't know. (*He picks up two glasses of beer, moves to Johnny, hands him a glass then moves down* L)

MIKE. What do you mean by that?

CALICO (*picking up her glass and moving down* R; *quickly*) He means nothing. Little Dave's in a bad temper, aren't you, Davey?

JOHNNY (*crossing to* R *of the table*) What's he in a bad temper about?

DAVE. Nothing. Come on, let's have a drink. (*He sits moodily in the easy chair down* L)

(MIKE *sits above the table.* JOHNNY *sits* R *of the table*)

JOHNNY. What're we drinking to?

MIKE. We don't need an excuse. (*He raises his glass*) To Calico. To the prettiest girl in the world.

CALICO (*raising her glass*) To the future.
DAVE. What's good about the future?

(CALICO *moves* C)

JOHNNY. The future's always good. It's bright and brilliant and wonderful. The present's lousy. But the future—that's terrific.
MIKE. To the future.
CALICO. Johnny's right. Here we go.

(*They drink enthusiastically.* DAVE *remains gloomy*)

JOHNNY. Dave, you're a misery. What's the matter with you?
DAVE. Nothing's the matter.
MIKE. Oh, never mind him. He sulks. He's like an old woman.

(CALICO *crosses to the easy chair* LC *and sits*)

DAVE. Why don't you leave me alone?
MIKE. You never know how he'll be next. He's either up or down. According to the moon.
CALICO (*laughing*) Poor Davey!
MIKE (*encouraged*) One day he's all right, the next he's got a sore tail. One day he's so mean he won't give you the right time. Next day he'll give you all he's got. He's queer.
CALICO. He's all right. Aren't you, Dave?
MIKE (*to Calico*) Show Johnny the birthday present Dave bought you. (*To Johnny*) That's the way he is.

(JOHNNY *rises and looks at Calico*)

He gave her a birthday present that took his whole week's wage.
DAVE. Why don't you shut up?
JOHNNY (*crossing to Calico*) What did he give you, Calico?
MIKE. Go on. Show him.

(CALICO *extends her left arm.* JOHNNY *pretends to examine the watch for the first time*)

It's good, isn't it?
JOHNNY. Yes. It's good.
CALICO. They're like real diamonds, aren't they?
JOHNNY. Yes. You'd say they were real.

(JOHNNY *catches* DAVE'S *eye*)

MIKE. You can't tell real ones from fake, I say.
JOHNNY. I don't agree. (*He looks at Calico*) If you look hard enough you can usually pick out a fake. (*He moves up* C)
MIKE (*rising*) Let's have another drink. (*He opens some more bottles of beer*)
CALICO (*rising*) Now you're talking. (*She moves to the table, picks up one of the opened bottles and gives it to Johnny*) Let's drink to the Farrell boys. They're all together again.

MIKE (*refilling his glass*) That's it. The Farrell boys.

(JOHNNY *refills his glass*)

CALICO. The big one—the little one—and the—the smart one.

(*She collects a bottle of beer, moves to Dave and shares it with him*)

JOHNNY (*putting the bottle on the table*) The mediocre one.

(*They drink*)

MIKE (*enjoying himself; to Johnny*) Tomorrow we'll get you a job. You can work in the yard with me. (*He sits above the table*) It'll toughen you up. (*To Calico*) He's been living in the lap of luxury.

CALICO. Maybe he'd rather push a pen like Dave.

JOHNNY (*sitting L of the table*) If it's a very small pen.

MIKE (*to Dave*) Can you fix it for him to get an office job?

DAVE. He doesn't want one.

JOHNNY. I'll look around first.

CALICO (*crossing above the table to the sideboard*) The way Lord Nelson did. With one eye. (*She puts the bottle on the sideboard*)

MIKE. Dave's where the money is. He's cute.

JOHNNY (*thoughtfully*) Is that so? What do you do, Dave?

MIKE. He pays wages. He's there first.

JOHNNY. Yes. (*He suddenly smiles*) Why don't we break in and walk out with the wages? Everybody's wages. That way I'll get my thousand pounds.

MIKE (*laughing*) That's a good idea.

CALICO (*moving RC*) What thousand pounds?

JOHNNY. The thousand I owe, darling.

(CALICO *moves up* C)

I'm a man of substance, you know. I don't get along on pin money. I owe it all over the place.

(*They drink.* DAVE *is thoughtful*)

DAVE (*to Johnny; very seriously*) You wouldn't get away with it. You wouldn't have a chance.

JOHNNY (*surprised*) What are you talking about?

DAVE. You said break into Mallaby's. You couldn't.

(CALICO *moves down* C)

MIKE. He was kidding, you chump.

CALICO (*moving down* R) He thought you were serious.

(*They laugh at* DAVE'S *discomfiture, then there is a silence*)

MIKE (*presently*) Do you suppose . . . ?

JOHNNY. What?

MIKE. Nothing.

DAVE. It's surprising nobody tried it. It could be done.

CALICO. How?

DAVE (*excitedly*) They collect the money from the bank on Thursday. Well, supposing . . .

JOHNNY. Supposing we drop the subject.

DAVE. I was only saying it's possible.

JOHNNY. It's dangerous talk.

MIKE. Yes. Shut up.

JOHNNY. It doesn't lead anywhere.

CALICO (*putting her glass on the sideboard*) Could be . . . (*She crosses to the easy chair LC*)

JOHNNY (*to Mike*) Do you think the old girl who runs this magnificent hotel could put me up, Mike? I've got to sleep somewhere.

(CALICO *sits on the right arm of the easy chair LC*)

CALICO. There's a place in the attic.

JOHNNY. It'll do.

MIKE. I'll go and ask her.

JOHNNY. I'll go with you. My bag's downstairs.

MIKE. How about another drink?

JOHNNY. Not me. I'm sleepy.

MIKE (*rising*) Come on.

(JOHNNY *rises*)

We'll go and see Mrs Finnegan.

(MIKE *and* JOHNNY *move to the door down* R)

CALICO. The Finnegans are sure to look after the Farrells.

JOHNNY. The nearest we've been to Ireland is singing *Phil the Fluter's Ball*. Good night.

CALICO. Good night, Johnny.

(MIKE *and* JOHNNY *exit down* R. DAVE *rises and stands facing the fireplace*)

(*She looks at her watch*) Johnny thinks the watch is good. Do you know, Dave, he valued it at nearly two hundred pounds.

DAVE (*strained*) That's silly. (*He turns, crosses above the table and stands down* RC)

CALICO (*rising and moving to* L *of Dave*) Yeah? Where d'you get all that money, Dave?

DAVE. It didn't cost . . . (*He takes her in his arms*) What if it did? You know I'm in love with you, Calico. You know that. If I'd the moon you could have that, too.

CALICO (*smiling and stroking his hair*) You're cute, Dave. That's really nice of you. (*She kisses him, then turns away*) But I wouldn't want you to get into trouble.

DAVE (*excitedly*) I don't care. So long as you . . . You do love me, don't you, Calico? I couldn't bear . . .

B

CALICO (*moving above the table*) There now. Take it easy. Of course I do.

DAVE. Then nothing else matters. Don't you see?

CALICO (*quietening him*) Yes. I understand. But Mike mustn't know, must he? (*She smiles vaguely, an indeterminate "Mona Lisa" smile*) Mike's nice, but . . .

DAVE. He's coarse, and crude, and rough. (*He moves to L of the table*) He isn't for you, Calico.

CALICO. Sure.

DAVE (*alarmed*) You're not falling for him?

CALICO. No. I'm all for you, Dave.

DAVE (*sighing*) I love you so much, Calico.

CALICO. Sure you do. (*Suddenly thoughtful*) Say—the other one—Johnny—he's okay, isn't he? He's cute.

CALICO *smiles as—*

the CURTAIN *falls*

SCENE 2

SCENE—*The same. An evening three weeks later.*

When the CURTAIN *rises* JOHNNY *is seated above the table, reading a racing journal. He appears reasonably satisfied. After turning a few pages he calls out to* DAVE, *who is in the bedroom.*

JOHNNY (*shouting*) What time does Cohen get to his office?

(*There is no reply*)

(*He glances round at the door up* R *and calls again*) Dave!

(DAVE *enters up* R, *in his shirt sleeves. He is nervous and strained*)

I thought you'd gone to bed. I've got a good thing here. What time can I contact Cohen?

DAVE. Still finding winners?

JOHNNY. I asked for information. Not sarcasm.

DAVE (*moving* C) Cohen's always there.

JOHNNY. He doesn't sleep there, does he?

DAVE. He doesn't sleep.

JOHNNY. I see.

DAVE. What have you got?

JOHNNY. "Red Timothy" for the first race. Looks good.

DAVE. They all look good.

JOHNNY (*carefully; surprised*) No, they don't. Usually they look bad. What's worrying *you*?

DAVE (*crossing to the fireplace*) You've been here three weeks and all you do is back horses.

JOHNNY. I don't back horses. I back winners.

DAVE (*moodily*) Some of the time.

JOHNNY. I'm not God. I don't read tomorrow's newspaper. Sometimes I'm wrong.

DAVE. Sometimes.

JOHNNY. I've paid my way, haven't I? It's better than pushing a pen for six-ten a week, like you do. What's getting into you? You criticize Mike, and you criticize me. (*He rises and moves down* LC) There must be something wrong with us—or something wonderful about you. Which is it?

(DAVE *starts, tightens his fist and advances earnestly a step or two towards Johnny*)

DAVE. I can answer that. Easily.

JOHNNY. Let's have it.

DAVE. It's us. We're no good, Johnny. Mike's a big ignorant fool. You bury your head in racing papers and dream big dreams. And me . . .

JOHNNY. Yes. What about you?

DAVE. You're giants at the side of me. (*He suggests height with a move of his hand. Quickly*) No, I don't mean this way. (*He moves up* C) I mean—Johnny, I'm . . .

JOHNNY. What the devil's wrong with you?

DAVE (*moving down* C) Johnny, I'm in a hell of a mess. I've got to tell somebody about it.

JOHNNY (*facing Dave*) Tell me.

DAVE. It's not easy.

JOHNNY (*shrugging*) Then don't tell me.

DAVE. Yes. I'll tell you. Johnny, it's . . . (*He breaks off*)

JOHNNY. It's about Calico, isn't it?

DAVE. You know about her . . .

JOHNNY. Not much. I know you bought her a present that cost you a whole week's wages.

DAVE. A week? If that was all.

JOHNNY. What *did* it cost?

DAVE. A fortune. It cost a fortune.

JOHNNY. A hundred and fifty?

DAVE. A hundred and sixty-five. That's what I wanted to tell you about, Johnny. Not just that, but . . .

JOHNNY. Where did you get the money?

DAVE. I—I . . .

JOHNNY. You're an accountant, aren't you?

DAVE. No. But I'm in the office.

JOHNNY. You handle the cash at Mallaby's?

DAVE. Yes.

JOHNNY. Is that where it came from?

DAVE. Yes. Not only that. More besides.

JOHNNY. How much?

DAVE. About three hundred altogether.

JOHNNY. Hell!

DAVE. Johnny, they'll find out the week after next I rigged the books. (*He crosses to the fireplace*) I tell you I'm in a hell of a mess.

JOHNNY. Didn't you know they'd find out?

DAVE. I didn't think about it. They were sure to. I was mad, I tell you. Absolutely cuckoo.

JOHNNY. About Calico? She's supposed to be Mike's girl, you know.

DAVE. I couldn't help it. She . . .

JOHNNY. Don't blame her. What are you going to do? What's the answer?

DAVE. I don't know. Johnny, I simply don't know. The auditors will be in and then . . .

JOHNNY (*moving* C) Jail. You ruddy little fool. For a girl like her.

DAVE. I know. She isn't worth it.

JOHNNY (*moving down* LC) She certainly isn't. And you're not worth fishing out of the sea. Are you sleeping with her?

DAVE (*aghast*) No. Honestly I'm not. You've got to believe me.

JOHNNY (*sitting in the easy chair* LC) I believe you. She'd be too smart.

DAVE. I'm not that low.

JOHNNY. Given the chance you would be.

DAVE. What am I to do?

JOHNNY. There's always jail.

DAVE. I'll kill myself first.

JOHNNY. Not you. You won't kill yourself. You ought to.

DAVE. If there's no other way out, I will.

JOHNNY. Go ahead, then. It solves a difficulty. If you shoot yourself you'll be out of danger. I think it's a good idea.

DAVE. Calling me names won't help.

JOHNNY. Then don't talk like a fool. What do you want *me* to do?

DAVE. I want advice.

JOHNNY. All right. Get the watch back from her. Sell it. Return the money. It'll be a start.

DAVE. Johnny, I couldn't do that.

JOHNNY. She wouldn't give it to you, would she? The cheap little gold-digger. She'll hang on like a leech. She's got you by the short hairs. Her and the moonlight. Big eyes and a lazy drawling voice. She kisses you and the angels sing. One hand on your knee and the other in your pocket.

DAVE (*crossing to* L *of the table; angrily*) She's no good. I told you she was no good. There's just something about her.

JOHNNY. Nothing I'd touch with a barge-pole.

DAVE. Don't be too sure.

JOHNNY. What do you mean?

Dave. She doesn't really care about me. (*He sits* L *of the table*) Nor about Mike either.

Johnny. She's crazy about herself.

Dave. And you.

Johnny. Me? Don't be silly.

Dave. Yes, she is. I've seen her watching you. The way she never looked at me. Differently.

Johnny (*rising*) She wouldn't waste her time. I'm broke. (*He moves behind Dave*) Besides, I'm not a complete idiot. She's Mike's girl.

Dave. Is she?

Johnny. Technically. (*He circles* RC, *then stands by the sideboard*) We're talking in circles. What the hell are we going to do about *you?* Why I should bother, I don't know. But I suppose I shall.

Dave (*optimistically*) If there's a way out, you'll find it.

Johnny. Yes? Your confidence touches me. I can't even look after myself.

Dave. You're still broke?

Johnny (*crossing up* L) I'm paying my way. But I owe a thousand quid. And the boys I owe it to are not nice people. Not when you owe them money.

Dave. We're both in a mess.

Johnny. We're *all three* in a mess.

Dave. Mike's all right.

Johnny. He wants to get married, doesn't he? One thing you've got to understand—if I'm helping you out of this you've got to stay away from Calico. Right?

Dave. Yes—if she'll stay away from me.

Johnny (*moving behind Dave*) What are you—a glamour boy?

Dave (*rising and turning to Johnny; protestingly*) She ran after me in the first place. I didn't start it.

Johnny. You must have something I can't see.

Dave. It isn't easy to resist a girl like her.

Johnny. I could do it. I've had women that made her look like a bundle of rags. She isn't my type.

Dave. Looks have nothing to do with it. It's something inside her.

Johnny. Anyway, stay away from her. Or bottle up that fatal fascination of yours. Put it any way you like. But no more of it.

(Calico *enters down* R)

Calico (*brightly*) May I come in?

Johnny (*moving to the fireplace; curtly*) You are in, aren't you?

Calico. Hello, Dave. What's worrying our Johnny?

Dave. Nothing, Calico. Why?

Calico (*shrugging*) He doesn't like me. (*She moves down* RC) I suppose you only like some people some of the time, but there's no occasion to be rude all of the time.

JOHNNY. That's the way it affects me. If I don't like people I'm rude.

CALICO. If I don't like 'em I keep quiet.

DAVE (*to Calico*) I just told him about the fix I'm in. (*He pauses*) I had to tell him.

CALICO (*to Johnny*) So you're taking it out of me. (*She crosses and sits in the easy chair* LC)

JOHNNY. Nobody's taking anything out of you. Not without a hammer and chisel.

CALICO. Did I ask him to steal the money?

JOHNNY. Not above a whisper.

CALICO (*to Dave*) Why should he blame me? Who's he think he is? Tell him the truth. I didn't ask any favours.

DAVE (*moving up* C) I didn't say you did. (*To Johnny*) It's my own fault.

JOHNNY. Of course it is. It was Adam's fault he got kicked out of Eden.

CALICO (*to Dave*) You're wasting your breath asking him for help. He's just a smart Alex standing around being smart. He won't help you.

JOHNNY. But *you* can. Why don't you?

CALICO. What can *I* do?

JOHNNY. Give him the watch back. Let him sell it. It's a start.

DAVE. It won't put it all back.

JOHNNY (*to Calico*) Well, how about it?

CALICO. Of course he can have it back.

(JOHNNY *is startled.* DAVE *moves down* C)

I was going to suggest it.

JOHNNY. Well—where is it?

CALICO. I'll get it tomorrow.

JOHNNY. Why not now?

CALICO. I haven't got it.

(JOHNNY *crosses above the table and stands up* R)

It's in my cubicle at the dance hall. (*To Dave*) Come with me in the morning and you can take it right away. Maybe that'll answer *him.*

JOHNNY (*defensively*) When he gets it I'll apologize.

CALICO. Meaning you don't think he will.

JOHNNY. Meaning I'm waiting until tomorrow to find out.

CALICO. He'll get it all right. Don't worry. Does Mike know?

DAVE. No.

JOHNNY. He hasn't got to know.

(MIKE *enters down* R)

MIKE (*smiling*) There you are, Calico. (*He crosses to Calico and embraces her*)

(JOHNNY *and* DAVE *watch* MIKE's *exuberance with blank faces*)

(*He moves to the sideboard*) Let's all have a drink.

JOHNNY. Not me. I'm going out.

MIKE (*transferring two bottles of beer and four glasses to the table*) Why not a drink? (*To Dave*) Get that perishing bottle of sherry. (*To Calico*) He's hoarding it. He talks about it, but we never see it.

JOHNNY. Dave's going with me. There's something we want to talk over.

MIKE (*moving to Calico*) It can wait, can't it? (*He hugs Calico from behind*) Hell, it isn't often we're all together.

JOHNNY. Dave wants to fix me up at Mallaby's. I'm sick of playing around.

MIKE. Of all the talk. You can do that in the morning.

JOHNNY. We're going now.

MIKE (*smiling*) You're not, you know. We're going to have a drink.

JOHNNY (*angrily*) We—are—not—going—to—have—a—drink.

(*There is an awkward silence.* MIKE *crosses to the fireplace*)

CALICO (*to Mike*) Let them go, Mike. They want to be alone. Let you and me have a drink.

MIKE (*refusing to be sidetracked*) What's the matter? What are you shouting about?

JOHNNY. If we say we're going out we mean it, that's all.

MIKE. You don't have to shout my head off.

JOHNNY. It's the only way to get an idea to penetrate. We're going out. That's simple enough, isn't it? Out.

CALICO (*rising; on a sudden thought*) They're upset, Mike. Don't argue with them.

MIKE. I don't like being yelled at.

JOHNNY (*moving to the door down* R) Come on, Dave. Let's go.

(DAVE *follows Johnny down* R)

CALICO (*to Johnny*) That's no solution. (*She moves to Mike*) Why don't you tell Mike what's on your mind?

MIKE. What *is* on your mind?

CALICO. Tell him. (*To Mike*) He isn't mad at you, Mike. It's me. Me and Dave. Dave's in a mess. A heck of a mess.

DAVE (*to Johnny*) Let's go.

JOHNNY (*fascinated*) Wait! Go on, Calico. Go on.

CALICO (*to Mike*) You might as well know now as later. You've got to know, anyway.

MIKE. What's everybody being so mysterious about?

CALICO. Now take it easy, Mike. You're always ready to go up in smoke. It's about Dave. He's in a jam.

MIKE (*irritated*) You said that before.

CALICO (*fingering Mike's tie*) The present he bought me—the watch. We thought it cost a whole week's wages. Mike, it cost more than that. It cost a hundred pounds.

MIKE (*aghast*) It what?

JOHNNY. You heard what she said.

MIKE. He never had so much money in his life.

JOHNNY. Oh, yes, he did.

CALICO. I'm trying to tell you.

MIKE. Is this someone's idea of being funny?

CALICO. Listen, Mike. It cost a hundred pounds.

DAVE (*crossing to LC; with bravado*) Nearly two hundred. She's trying to tell you I got it from Mallaby's and they don't know about it yet.

MIKE (*dangerously*) You took it from Mallaby's?

CALICO. Go easy, Mike.

MIKE. They don't know.

JOHNNY. But they soon will.

MIKE (*pushing Calico aside and crossing to Dave*) You fool! You bloody little fool! (*He seizes Dave by the shoulders and vigorously shakes him*)

JOHNNY (*crossing to C*) That won't help. Let go of him.

(MIKE, *as if dazed, releases* DAVE, *who moves up* R)

He may not be worth it, but we've got to help him.

MIKE. Why the hell did he do it? (*To Dave*) What for?

CALICO. It's tough, handling all that money. Nobody should be paid what he's paid and given all that money to play around with. There ought to be a law.

MIKE (*vaguely*) It wasn't his.

JOHNNY (*mockingly*) No, we know that. But he took it. And he can't go to jail, can he?

MIKE (*angrily*) Why not? Why can't he?

JOHNNY (*shrugging*) If you look at it that way . . .

MIKE. It'll do him good.

CALICO. Mike, this isn't *you* talking. If it is I don't know you.

MIKE (*moving up* C) Nobody knows anybody. I don't know him (*On a sudden thought*) Why did you pay all that for a watch? Of all the brainless things to do. Why?

JOHNNY (*quickly interceding*) That isn't all. (*He moves* RC) He borrowed more than that.

MIKE (*ironically*) Borrowed?

JOHNNY (*crossing to the easy chair* LC; *amused*) Borrowed. (*He sits on the right arm of the easy chair*) He owes more than that.

MIKE. How much? (*To Dave*) How much did you steal?

DAVE. I *stole* a few hundred.

JOHNNY. Not many hundreds, you see. Just a few.

MIKE. All right. It's his own affair. He can go to jail. He can stew in his own juice.

CALICO. No, he can't.

JOHNNY. We've got our reputation to consider.

DAVE. What reputation?

JOHNNY. Our pure and unsullied family name, you dope.

MIKE. And that's nothing to be sneered at. (*He crosses to the sideboard. To Dave*) A chump like you can get the whole crowd of us talked about.

DAVE (*referring to Johnny*) He owes more than I owe. I suppose that's a debt of honour.

JOHNNY. It'll be paid.

DAVE. How?

CALICO. I know how.

JOHNNY. If you do you're a genius. Let's hear it.

CALICO. The trouble with you boys is you're sitting on a volcano all the time. You're like three kettles always on the gas. You can't tell which of you'll start boiling first. (*She sits in the easy chair down* L) All you know is—any time on the clock—one of you's going to get steamed up and boil over.

JOHNNY (*to Mike*) She means we're quarrelsome.

CALICO. At least Dave had guts. He got sick of handling other folks' money. So he took some.

MIKE (*moving down* R) Is that showing guts?

CALICO. Yes, it is. What do *you* do? (*She refers to Johnny*) What does *he* do?

JOHNNY. Well, what *do* we do?

CALICO. *You* get your money the sneaky way. You bet with money you don't have. Then, when you lose, you crawl out the back way and play hard-to-find. That's pretty brave, isn't it?

JOHNNY. They'll get it back.

CALICO (*rising*) Yes?

JOHNNY. Anybody who can take a rise out of a bookie isn't doing anything criminal, anyway.

CALICO. No. It's safe enough. But it's gutless. (*She moves below the table. To Mike*) And as for you, you've no right to call Dave any hard names. You talk bigger than he does. You're all talk.

MIKE (*outraged*) Well, I . . .

CALICO (*mockingly*) "One of these days I'll take you on a cruise to the Mediterranean, darling. One of these days I'll buy the best house in town, and we'll get married, darling, and so-on and so-on, darling." But what do you *do* about it? (*She moves up* R)

(MIKE *is silent*. JOHNNY *is disgusted*)

JOHNNY. What *can* he do?

CALICO (*after a pause*) Dave did something, didn't he? (*She crosses to the fireplace*) And don't tell me to look where it got him. I know. He's in a jam. But he needn't be. He can be got out.

DAVE. How? How, Calico?

CALICO (*mysteriously*) It can be done.

DAVE (*eagerly*) How?

CALICO (*sitting in the easy chair down* L; *to Dave*) If they'd half the guts you have they could get you out. And put themselves in clover, too.

JOHNNY. He says, "How?" Why don't you answer him? And while you're about it you can tell me, too.

MIKE (*crossing to Calico; subdued*) What are you talking about, Calico?

CALICO. I daren't tell you. You just *look* rugged.

DAVE. If there's any way out . . .

(MIKE *moves to the fireplace*)

CALICO. Of course there's a way out.

JOHNNY. To her it's easy. She's a genius.

CALICO. Yes, it's easy, too. I know what I'm saying.

JOHNNY. I wish *I* did. Let's have it. I'm palpitating with excitement.

(CALICO *looks musingly at first one and then the other*)

CALICO (*gently, almost whimsically*) Dave stole the money from Mallaby's. (*She rises and crosses to* C) He took it out of the wages money; but they don't know yet, because he altered his figures in his books. Soon they'll find out his figures don't tally with his cash. All right, but supposing someone broke into the place the night before pay-day and took the entire caboodle. His books wouldn't have to balance, would they? No one would know how much had been taken. Two thousand pounds and a couple of hundreds. See what I mean?

(*The others stare at Calico in shocked silence. Finally,* JOHNNY *laughs incredulously and mirthlessly, and flops off the arm into the chair*)

MIKE. Calico—you don't know what you're saying.

CALICO. Oh, yes, I do. It'd put Dave in the clear. It'd put Johnny straight with his bookie friends. And—oh, Mike, you know what it'd mean to us. (*She crosses to Mike, takes his hand in hers and gazes earnestly at him*) We could do all the things we've talked about. A home . . . You want to marry me, don't you?

MIKE. Yes, but . . .

JOHNNY (*rising and crossing down* RC) If he falls for that he ought to *be* in a home. Segregated. Think again, darling.

CALICO (*crossing to* L *of Johnny*) You don't like the idea, do you?

JOHNNY. That's putting it mildly.

CALICO. Are you too honest to steal? Or too scared?

JOHNNY. I'm not scared.

CALICO. You're not too honest to welsh on a bet.

JOHNNY. Jail doesn't frighten me. It just isn't attractive.

CALICO. One of these days a tough bookmaker's going to send

a strongarm boy down here to push your face back. Isn't that right?

JOHNNY. It's possible.

CALICO. Break into Mallaby's and you can pay it. You've even got a good alibi for the money. You're a racing man. Everybody knows that. You visit the tracks and win, don't you?

JOHNNY. Once in a while.

CALICO. So that accounts for your having the cash. You picked the right horses.

JOHNNY. It's a good alibi for the money. But I've no alibi for being caught with my hand in the till.

CALICO. You're intelligent. Sometimes you're bright. You could plan it. (*She moves up* C *to Dave*) Dave, Mallaby's draw money from the bank on Thursdays and keep it overnight, don't they?

DAVE. Some of it. About half. They pick up the other half Friday morning.

CALICO. Is there any special guard?

DAVE. No. Only a night watchman. He's there every night.

CALICO. Do you know him?

DAVE. We all know him. (*He moves to* L *of Johnny*) It's old Joe Ryan. We've known him all our lives.

CALICO. You say he's old?

DAVE. Well—sixtyish.

CALICO (*moving down* C) Would it be impossible to break in?

DAVE. No. It could be done.

CALICO. Is it worth thinking over? Am I crazy?

JOHNNY. Which question shall we answer first?

MIKE. You're serious, aren't you?

CALICO. Sure I am. Why not?

JOHNNY (*crossing to* R *of Calico*) You're a little beauty, aren't you? You certainly are a prize-winner.

CALICO (*crossing to Mike*) What d'you say, Mike?

MIKE (*hesitantly*) I never did anything like that.

JOHNNY (*to Mike*) Don't listen to her. If you do you're a bigger fool than I took you for.

CALICO. Think it over, Mike. (*She reaches up and kisses him very encouragingly, preparatory to leaving*) Dave needs the money or he goes to jail. (*She crosses to* C) Johnny needs it or one dark night he'll get his pretty face knocked out of shape. It's up to you, Mike, to decide whether *you* need the money. (*She crosses to the door down* R) We can't travel far without, can we? Think it over, boys. I'll see you in the morning.

(CALICO *exits down* R. *The others stand awkwardly for a few moments, then* JOHNNY *moves to the table and pours three glasses of beer. As if relieved by the thought of liquor, each reaches for a glass*)

JOHNNY. There goes a woman. And what a woman. (*To Mike*) You certainly picked a beauty.

MIKE. Shut up.

JOHNNY (*moving up* C) When a man marries he's inviting trouble for himself. (*He takes his hat and coat from the hooks and moves down* C) But you picked a woman who's going to land the entire family in jail.

MIKE. I said "shut up".

JOHNNY (*moving to the door down* R) Oh, that girl! (*He opens the door*)

MIKE. You said enough about her. I don't like it. Why don't you shut up?

JOHNNY (*closing the door; after a pause*) Are we to gather from your attitude that you're beginning to weaken?

MIKE. You're not to gather anything. I don't know.

JOHNNY (*moving* RC) Indecision! He doesn't know. Well, I do. You can include me out.

DAVE. But, Johnny . . .

JOHNNY. I'm not entirely mad.

DAVE. I thought you'd think of something—some way out. All you do is crab everything.

JOHNNY. Do *you* think it's a smart suggestion? For us, I mean? We're amateurs. What do we know about burglary? We wouldn't get away with it. We couldn't.

MIKE (*vaguely*) We might.

JOHNNY (*staring at Mike*) Hell's bells, she's got you on the run. She calls the tune and you dance. Well, not me. She isn't *my* girl. (*He moves to the door down* R *and opens it*) You're welcome to her and the devilry she conjures up in you. Good night.

DAVE (*moving down* R; *appealing*) Johnny . . .

JOHNNY. Good night.

(JOHNNY *exits down* R. MIKE *pours himself another drink*)

MIKE. You got us into a fine mess, didn't you? Why didn't you think twice before you did it?

DAVE (*despairingly*) Why didn't I think *once*?

(*There is a thoughtful silence*)

MIKE. And by the way, why in blazes did you spend all that money on a present for Calico? What was your idea?

DAVE (*crossing down* L) Just—I had the money. I'd taken it. I had to spend it. And I saw the watch. It was a beautiful watch.

MIKE (*grunting*) It was a fool thing to do.

DAVE (*sitting in the easy chair down* L) Yes. I know now, when it's too late. (*He buries his face in his hands. After a pause*) Mike, I don't want to go to jail. I don't think I could stand it. Shut up in a cell I'd go mad.

MIKE. You won't go to jail.

DAVE. Yes, I will. You see—I will.

MIKE. No.

DAVE. What's going to stop me? You heard what Johnny had to say. (*He is in tears*)

MIKE (*crossing to Dave*) He'll come round. (*He puts a friendly hand on Dave's shoulder*) I don't know what made Calico say what she did. Break into Mallaby's—it's not right. It's a bad thing.

DAVE (*looking up eagerly*) It could be done, Mike.

MIKE. I don't know. Perhaps so. Perhaps not. I don't know, Dave.

DAVE. If only Johnny would help. He's got brains. He could work out a plan.

MIKE. You didn't suggest this to her, did you?

DAVE. Honest to God I didn't, Mike. I don't know how she thought of it. (*Shrewdly*) She said it was the only way you could afford to be married. It is, too, Mike. You could do anything with a third share.

MIKE (*weakening*) We could go abroad. (*He moves LC. Freezing*) But I don't like it. It's wrong.

(DAVE *rises, moves up L, shrugs resignedly, and looks calculatingly at Mike*)

DAVE. Otherwise you'll lose her. She's attractive. There are other men who want her.

(JOHNNY *enters down R. His mood is quieter. He crosses to the table and pours a drink for himself*)

MIKE. You said good night.

JOHNNY. Dave, I'll help you one way or another. I'll have to.

(DAVE *moves to L of the table*)

I promised Ma I'd help you. But you certainly make it hard.

DAVE (*eagerly*) You could plan it, Johnny. I knew you would.

JOHNNY. I could plan what?

DAVE (*as if surprised*) Mallaby's. What Calico suggested. You've got ideas. With you behind us we'd do it easy.

JOHNNY (*crossing down L*) No. No, Dave, not that. Some other way.

MIKE. What other way?

JOHNNY. I'll think of something. Another drink, Mike. (*He moves to the table and refills Mike's glass*) Perhaps we could . . .

DAVE. What?

JOHNNY (*crossing down R*) No, not that either.

(DAVE *moves to the divan and sits*)

I've got to think.

MIKE. You've got to think fast.

JOHNNY (*to Dave*) When do you expect the auditors?

DAVE. A couple of weeks. There isn't much time.

JOHNNY (*thoughtfully surveying his glass*) Imagine old Joe Ryan being night watchman at Mallaby's. His son was in my class at school. Old Joe's as deaf as a post.

(DAVE *rises*)

(*He crosses and sits above the table*) He'll be no good as a night watchman. He wouldn't hear a bomb explode.

MIKE (*moving to* L *of the table*) That'd make it easier, wouldn't it?

JOHNNY. I guess so.

MIKE. Dave knows the office inside out. We'd know just where to put our hands on everything.

DAVE (*moving to* R *of the table*) It would be like shelling peas, Johnny. I know the building. I could even get the keys.

JOHNNY. We could make impressions of the keys.

DAVE. Then they might suspect me.

JOHNNY. They couldn't prove anything. (*Confidently*) I could plan it. I could think of a way.

DAVE (*eagerly*) You'll do it, Johnny.

(JOHNNY *is suddenly serious. Just as suddenly he gives way to a smile*)

JOHNNY. Yes, damn you, Dave, I'll go to work on the idea.

DAVE (*sitting* R *of the table*) Johnny, I knew you would.

(MIKE *sits* L *of the table and refills the glasses. The* CURTAIN *begins to fall*)

JOHNNY. Mind you, it's got to be planned thoroughly. No mistakes. We can't afford any. We've got to plan it like a military campaign. Now listen to this for a start. Here's what I've been thinking . . .

the CURTAIN *falls*

ACT II

SCENE—*The same. Morning, a fortnight later.*

When the CURTAIN *rises,* CALICO *is standing by the window, holding the edge of the curtain in one hand. She glances at her watch, then moves slowly to the table* C, *takes a cigarette from the packet on it, and lights it. She is nervous.* JOHNNY *enters down* R. CALICO, *startled, turns, but recovers when she sees Johnny.*

JOHNNY. Anything happen?

CALICO. Not a thing?

JOHNNY *(equally tense)* I thought we'd have heard something before now. *(He crosses to the table and takes a cigarette from the packet)* Where's Mike?

*(*CALICO *indicates the bedroom door up* R)

CALICO *(moving to the window)* Maybe you were wrong?

JOHNNY *(off-handed)* How?

CALICO. Maybe the man didn't see you.

JOHNNY. You can see me, can't you? He was as near as that.

CALICO. Maybe he was short-sighted.

JOHNNY. The lights were full on, I tell you. He couldn't miss seeing us. *(He lights his cigarette)*

*(*MIKE *enters up* R)

MIKE. Johnny—Johnny, what do you make of it?

JOHNNY. Make of what?

MIKE. This. Nothing happening.

JOHNNY. I don't know.

MIKE. I thought . . .

JOHNNY *(crossing to the fireplace)* I just don't understand.

CALICO. You didn't recognize the old man. Why should he recognize you?

JOHNNY *(very impatient)* Please don't be stupid. He can describe us, can't he? They can have us paraded in front of him, can't they?

CALICO. It's two nights ago. Why haven't they?

JOHNNY. How the devil do I know?

MIKE· *(moving above the table)* Johnny thinks they'll arrest us and let him look us over.

JOHNNY. Certainly. They're not fools.

CALICO *(moving to* R *of the table)* I think he didn't see you.

JOHNNY. Oh, God! *(Sarcastically)* That's right. The old fool just stood there and stared at us. He looked at Mike. He said, "You've killed him". We all stood there paralysed for half a minute. But she thinks he didn't see us.

CALICO. Who was he?

MIKE (*sitting above the table*) I never saw him before.

JOHNNY (*moving behind the easy chair* LC) What does it matter? (*He crosses to* C) Perhaps for the first time in ten years Joe Ryan was lonely and had a pal to sit up with him. That's the night we decided to be burglars. Joe Ryan was as deaf as a post, but he heard us all right. He came on us like a ghost. "What *you* doing here?" he said. (*He crosses to the fireplace*) This genius here—(*he indicates Mike*) gave him the answer.

MIKE. I didn't know . . .

JOHNNY. He decided he'd be tough, so he carried a gun. Where he got it from I don't know. By the way, where *did* you get it from?

MIKE. I only meant to scare him.

JOHNNY. You did that all right. Straight through the brain. Dead as a door-nail. A beauty. A bull's-eye. (*He sits in the easy chair down* L) Clever boy. He thought fast, you see. Marvellous co-ordination of brain and muscle. Joe went out like a light.

MIKE. I didn't mean to kill him.

JOHNNY. Just scare him.

MIKE. He put all the lights on. He knew us. He recognized Dave and me. If I hadn't shot him we'd be in jail now.

JOHNNY. But not for murder.

CALICO (*crossing down* L) What happened then?

JOHNNY. We all sort of stared at each other. It was like an atom bomb, it made such a hell of a noise. Joe was on the floor. And then—suddenly—there was the old man.

MIKE. He walked in at the doorway.

JOHNNY. He looked at us. He said, "You've killed him".

CALICO. Then what?

JOHNNY. We got out as fast as we could.

CALICO. Didn't he try to stop you?

JOHNNY. No. (*He rises, moves to the fireplace and stands facing it*) I've told you a dozen times. He just stood there.

MIKE. He was an old man. Older than Joe Ryan. He couldn't have stopped us.

JOHNNY (*turning and moving up* L *of the table*) He was a hundred years old. There were only three of us. But if he'd started anything genius here would have shot him.

MIKE (*weary of sarcasm*) He's frightened. He gets sarcastic when he's frightened.

JOHNNY (*moving to the sideboard*) Certainly I'm frightened. So would you be if you'd any imagination—or brains.

CALICO. Getting excited isn't going to help.

JOHNNY (*moving down* R) Nothing's going to help.

CALICO. One thing might.

JOHNNY. Name it.

CALICO (*sitting in the easy chair* LC) Keeping our heads. Supposing it's true what you say . . .

JOHNNY. It is true.

CALICO. Anybody'd think he wanted it to be true. All right, suppose it is. What's the first thing the police would do? He described the men he saw. How long would it take them to suspect you?

MIKE. Five minutes. They'd know it was someone who knew the place. They'd suspect Dave right away. Then me.

CALICO. But they haven't suspected you yet, or they'd have been around to see you.

JOHNNY. That's why I'm frightened. It's—it's odd.

CALICO. You'd rather they arrested you?

JOHNNY. Let me tell you. (*He crosses to* C) I'm no more a coward than the next man. If they'd come straight here and arrested me I'd have taken it on the chin and not burst into tears. I'd have understood it. But this—this I don't understand. (*He crosses to the fireplace*) It's like a ghost, and ghosts terrify me. It's something I can't lay a finger on. Why? Why doesn't something happen?

CALICO. There's only one answer. The old man didn't recognize you.

JOHNNY (*crossing to* C) God, she's going into that again. (*He moves up* LC. *To Mike*) You tell her. Tell her in simple language exactly how it happened.

(JOHNNY *crosses and exits up* R)

MIKE. I didn't think he'd take it like this.

CALICO. No.

MIKE. Dave, perhaps, but not Johnny.

CALICO. He's not so frightened as to show us how much money he got.

MIKE. How do you mean?

CALICO. Have you seen any?

MIKE. I don't want to.

CALICO. That was the idea, wasn't it?

MIKE. Johnny hid it.

CALICO. How much?

MIKE. I don't know. He'd stuffed a few wads of notes in his pockets. We cleared out pretty quickly. I didn't get any money.

CALICO (*rising and moving up* C) But Johnny did. You want your share.

MIKE. I don't—think I do.

CALICO. Don't be a fool.

MIKE. Joe was a decent old stick. I'd known him all my life.

CALICO. Joe who?

MIKE. Ryan. The night-watchman. I shouldn't have shot him.

CALICO. It was an accident.

C

MIKE. I shouldn't have shot him.

CALICO (*moving up* R) Well, you did.

MIKE. Why did you give me the gun, Calico?

CALICO (*moving up* C) I—hell, I don't know.

MIKE. Where did you get it?

CALICO. A soldier. I don't know who he was.

MIKE. You shouldn't have given me it.

CALICO (*crossing to the fireplace*) You didn't have to kill him, did you? If you'd had any sense, I mean.

MIKE. No—if I'd had any sense.

CALICO. You could have threatened him.

MIKE. He recognized me.

CALICO. Is that why you pulled the trigger?

MIKE. I don't know. I hadn't a reason. It just happened. I wouldn't have hurt him for fifty thousand pounds. I wouldn't shoot a dog. But I shot old Joe. I'll hang for it, Calico.

CALICO. For heaven's sake!

MIKE. I will. We all will.

CALICO (*crossing down* R) Not if you keep your heads. They can't prove a thing. I've got a feeling. I know I'm right. If they could prove it they'd be here double quick. Dave's the one I'm worried about.

MIKE. Yes.

CALICO. Every morning he has to go to the office. It's the same room where it happened.

MIKE. That's true.

CALICO (*crossing above the table to the fireplace*) How long can he stand the strain?

MIKE. He'll have to give up his job.

CALICO. No. He mustn't do that. They'd know why.

MIKE. Dave was always nervous. As a kid. If they question him, he'll break down.

(*They are silent, considering this*)

CALICO. I feel like a drink.

MIKE (*rising and crossing to the sideboard*) I'll get it. (*He takes a bottle of beer and two glasses from the sideboard, moves to the table and pours the beer*)

(DAVE *enters down* R, *crosses to the table, picks up a glass and drinks from it.* CALICO *and* MIKE *look at him, but do not speak.*

JOHNNY *enters up* R. *They all stand and watch* DAVE, *who puts down the glass, sighs with exaggerated enjoyment, and smiles. It is not the Dave they have expected, nervy and shrunken, and they are bewildered by his apparent confidence*)

· DAVE. That's a beautiful beer. (*He examines the label on the beer bottle*) Oh-Be-Joyful. (*As if on a sudden thought, he moves to* L *of the table, turns and surveys them in turn*) But no one *is* joyful. Can anything be wrong?

MIKE (*sympathetically*) Dave!

DAVE. Yes, Mike?

MIKE. What happened. Dave?

DAVE. Where, Mike?

MIKE. At the office. Mallaby's.

DAVE. Oh, we got through quite a lot of work, Mike. We're organized, you know. Everything runs smoothly.

JOHNNY (*crossing to* C; *impatiently*) Did they say anything?

DAVE. Did who say anything?

JOHNNY. Stop being clever. Did anybody say anything?

DAVE. Let me see now. Mr Jenkinson remarked that it looked like rain, and I distinctly remember Mr Lee said he had toothache.

JOHNNY (*to Mike*) Did somebody say something funny, or am I slow on the uptake? (*To Dave*) Were the police there?

DAVE (*sitting* L *of the table*) Yes. (*His brightness now fades*)

(MIKE *stands above the table.* CALICO *moves to* L *of Dave*)

JOHNNY (*crossing and standing* L *of Mike*) Well?

CALICO (*with a hand on Dave's shoulder*) Tell us, Dave.

MIKE (*softly*) Tell us, Dave.

JOHNNY (*ironically*) Tell us, Dave. What's the matter with you all?

CALICO (*to Johnny*) Leave him alone, you fool. Can't you see . . . ?

(DAVE *sits facing front, one elbow on the table. His expression is vague and faraway*)

JOHNNY. Can't I see what?

CALICO (*moving to* R *of Dave and pushing Johnny aside*) Are you all right, Dave?

(JOHNNY, *realizing now that his own impatience is unwise, moves down* R. *They all survey Dave anxiously*)

DAVE. I was sick. They sent me home.

CALICO. Didn't they say anything about—about what had happened?

DAVE. They were nice to me. They told me to go home and I'd feel better in the morning.

MIKE. What did the police say?

DAVE. I didn't see them.

MIKE. Didn't they ask you any questions?

JOHNNY. How could they if he didn't see them?

CALICO. But the police were there, Dave. You said they were there.

DAVE. Yes. Yes, they were there.

CALICO. It's funny.

MIKE. What's funny?

CALICO. They didn't question Dave. (*To Johnny*) Do you still say the old man must have seen you?

(JOHNNY *has no reply to this*)

DAVE. That's what really *is* funny, you know.

CALICO } (*together*) { What?
MIKE } { What do you mean, Dave?

DAVE (*rising*) The old man's disappeared.

MIKE. Disappeared?

DAVE. Yes. .

JOHNNY. How do you mean, he's disappeared?

DAVE. I don't know.

JOHNNY. Who says so?

DAVE. I heard Mr D'Arcy say so. He was talking to Mr Ledgard—he's one of the directors.

CALICO. What did he say?

DAVE. He said the night watchman had a friend with him, an old chap from the other side of the town. But they don't know where he is.

JOHNNY. How the hell could that happen?

DAVE. I don't know.

JOHNNY. It's ridiculous.

MIKE. People don't disappear.

JOHNNY (*to Dave*) You mean no one's seen him since—since Thursday?

(DAVE *nods*)

(*He crosses to* C) But it's crazy. He just wouldn't do a thing like that.

MIKE. Perhaps he was afraid.

CALICO. Of what?

MIKE. Well, I don't know. Perhaps he was afraid they'd blame him. It could be.

JOHNNY (*crossing down* R) I don't believe it.

CALICO. Can you think of a better reason?

DAVE. They're searching all over town for him. They say when they find him they'll have the murderers.

JOHNNY (*looking at Calico*) They certainly will. But it's ridiculous. (*Appealing*) Don't you see? It's quite ridiculous. (*He crosses to the fireplace*) If I read it in a book I'd throw the book away. It couldn't happen. Witnesses don't vanish like that. There's something fishy about it.

CALICO. But it has happened.

JOHNNY. I don't believe it.

MIKE. Then why don't they do something?

JOHNNY. I don't know.

CALICO. It explains it, anyway.

JOHNNY. Not to my liking. I don't like it.

CALICO. You're not supposed to.

JOHNNY (*sitting in the easy chair down* L; *very thoughtfully*) I'm—not —supposed—to.

(*There is a knock on the door down* R. *They stiffen with apprehension.* DAVE *and* JOHNNY *rise.* CALICO *crosses to the door down* R, *opens it, exits and closes the door behind her. Not a word is spoken until the door is closed*)

MIKE. Who do you think? . . .

DAVE. Johnny . . .

JOHNNY (*crossing to* C) Now listen—no nerves. Answer questions easily. If it's true, if the old man's missing, they can't prove a thing. Keep hold of yourselves. That's what we have to do. Take it easy.

DAVE. I don't think I . . .

JOHNNY. Shut up!

(CALICO *enters down* L. *She closes the door, leans against it and blows with relief*)

Who was it?

CALICO. Somebody got the wrong room. Looking for Mrs Davies on the next floor.

MIKE (*sitting above the table*) I was scared stiff.

JOHNNY. So was I. (*Carefully*) We all were. And we haven't got to be. They can't prove anything. Calico was right. They can't prove it, unless we crack up and give the game away.

DAVE. I'd like another drink.

JOHNNY (*crossing to the fireplace*) Give him a drink, Mike.

MIKE. It's all finished.

DAVE (*crossing down* R) I feel rotten.

JOHNNY. Go and lie down.

DAVE. I want a drink.

JOHNNY. Where are you going?

DAVE. For a drink.

JOHNNY. I wouldn't go out if I were you.

DAVE. I'm going for a drink.

MIKE } (*together*) { Be careful, Dave.
CALICO } { Shall I come with you?

(DAVE, *without replying, exits down* R)

CALICO. Will he be all right?

JOHNNY. We can't tie him up. He'll have to be all right. (*He moves down* R) I wish I could see daylight.

MIKE (*as if bluntly hitting the nail on the head*) Perhaps he's dead.

(JOHNNY *crosses down* L)

CALICO. Perhaps who's dead.

MIKE. The old man.

CALICO. Joe Ryan's dead.

MIKE. No, the other one. The one who saw us.

CALICO. He wasn't dead then, was he?

MIKE. No, but—he could have had a heart attack.

CALICO. Don't be silly.

JOHNNY (*moving up* L; *after a pause*) The old man dead! Wait a minute. It's an idea.

CALICO. What sort of an idea?

JOHNNY (*moving to* L *of the table; excited*) That could be the answer. Is it possible?

CALICO. No.

(*The sound of the violin is heard off in the distance*)

JOHNNY (*to Calico*) Why not? He was as old as the Ancient Mariner.

CALICO. And he had a weak heart.

JOHNNY (*stubbornly*) Perhaps he had.

CALICO. Very convenient.

JOHNNY. It's possible.

CALICO. Would you believe that if you read it in a book?

JOHNNY (*moving up* R) You're too smart to live. Tell me this: if he's alive, why haven't they had us in front of him before now? They must suspect us. Why are they doing nothing?

CALICO. Dave says he's disappeared.

JOHNNY. That's likely, isn't it?

MIKE. I think I'm right. I think he's dead.

CALICO. Then everything's fine. (*She crosses and stands behind the easy chair* LC)

(*The sound of the violin grows gradually louder*)

JOHNNY. Perhaps it is. Yes, perhaps it is.

CALICO. I simply love a happy ending.

JOHNNY (*to Mike*) She's disappointed. She wants to see us hang.

(*They are silent. Outside the beggar plays his violin. The bow scrapes mournfully through the same tune: "If I Should Fall in Love Again"*)

JOHNNY. That blasted fiddle. Does he only know one tune?

CALICO. It's a good tune.

MIKE. He's been playing it for ten years.

JOHNNY. Always the same tune?

CALICO. He's got a one-track mind.

MIKE (*quoting*) "If I Should Fall in Love Again . . ."

JOHNNY (*moving down* R) You'd fall in love with her again, and we'd be in the same soup all over again.

MIKE (*rising*) I don't have to listen to talk like that, Johnny.

JOHNNY (*moving up* R) No. I'm sorry, Mike. I'm sorry.

(JOHNNY *exits suddenly up* R. *The sound of the violin fades into the distance*)

MIKE. Fancy Johnny saying that.

CALICO. He doesn't like me.

MIKE. I think he does.

CALICO. He has a queer way of showing it.

MIKE (*crossing to the fireplace*) No. He's upset, that's all. We're all upset. If we're not careful we'll be fighting among ourselves. Calico, couldn't we go away? Just you and me.

CALICO (*moving down* LC) Where to?

MIKE. Who cares? Anywhere.

CALICO. A slow boat to China. What'll we use for money?

MIKE. We have a little. Johnny had a few wads in his pockets.

CALICO. You said you wouldn't touch it.

MIKE. For you I would. (*He moves to Calico and attempts to embrace her*)

(CALICO *evades him*)

I'd do anything for you.

CALICO. There's a time and a place. This isn't either.

MIKE. I want you so much, Calico. I can't go on like this. Dave watching you with his greedy little eyes. I don't like to see it. Even Johnny.

CALICO (*quickly*) What about Johnny?

MIKE. I think he wants you, too.

(CALICO *is so fascinated by this theory that she is quiescent whilst* MIKE *caresses her*)

CALICO (*without conviction*) He hates the very sight of me.

MIKE. No, he doesn't. He knows you're my girl and I'd break his neck if he touched you even with his little finger. He doesn't hate you. He's like me, Calico. He goes from one extreme to the other. If he can't have you to love he tries to hate you. You know how I—feel about you, Calico. Let's go away together—anywhere to be together. (*He pulls her to him and kisses her*)

(CALICO, *as soon as she can, breaks away from him*)

CALICO. This isn't the time for love, Mike. We're in a shadow, not moonlight. What a time to talk about love—(*she crosses below him to the fireplace*) with a hangman's noose hanging over you.

MIKE (*quietly*) I killed a man for you, Calico.

CALICO (*turning; shocked*) Not for me, Mike.

MIKE. Who else?

(CALICO *is uneasily silent*)

I'm not blaming you, but I'm saying I wouldn't have done it for anyone on God's earth but you.

CALICO. You didn't do it for me. You did it to get me. It isn't the same thing.

MIKE (*moving to her*) Yes, to get you. And I want you, Calico. I . . .

CALICO (*sitting in the easy chair down* L) Isn't anything sacred? Not now, Mike.

MIKE. I'm making a fool of myself.

CALICO. I'm not in the mood, that's all. I . . .

MIKE. I'm just a fool.

CALICO. No. You're all right, Mike. You're wonderful. But you don't choose the best background, and your timing's out of this world.

MIKE (*crossing to* C) You mean I'm clumsy.

CALICO. Only in a nice way. Why don't you ask Johnny about the money? Talk's all right, but we'd need money to get out of the country.

MIKE. I'll ask him.

(MIKE *exits up* R, *leaving the door open. The sound of the violin grows louder. During the ensuing dialogue off,* CALICO *rises, moves to the table, pours the remains of the beer into a glass, drinks it, yawns, crosses to the divan and flings herself languidly on to it*)

JOHNNY (*off*) You're crazy, what put that idea into your head?

MIKE (*off*) We're supposed to share it, aren't we? I only want my share.

JOHNNY (*off*) Share it, share it, what do you think this is— Xmas? It's hidden, I tell you—the money's hidden.

MIKE (*off*) You've no call to shout, Johnny. I'm only asking for what's due to me.

(MIKE *and* JOHNNY *enter up* R. JOHNNY *crosses to* C *and confronts* Calico. MIKE *stands down* R. *The violin music ceases*)

JOHNNY (*to Calico*) I suppose this is your idea?

MIKE. It's my idea.

CALICO (*injured*) What's he talking about?

JOHNNY. As if you don't know. He wants us to share out the money we got from Mallaby's. Do you think that's smart?

MIKE Why not? I only want my share.

CALICO (*rising and crossing to the fireplace*) It doesn't concern me.

MIKE. I'm entitled to my share.

JOHNNY. Certainly you are. If it hadn't been for you we wouldn't have got anything at all. (*He moves up* R) Only six months in jail.

MIKE (*crossing to* R *of the table*) I want my share.

JOHNNY (*moving down* R) You can have it all—every penny.

MIKE. I don't want it all.

CALICO (*to Johnny*) What are you grumbling about, anyway?

JOHNNY (*with an effort*) All right. As I'm talking to a fool and a gold-digger I'll try to be patient.

(MIKE *moves threateningly towards Johnny, but* CALICO *intervenes*)

CALICO. Don't touch him.

MIKE. He isn't going to talk like that. I won't have it.

CALICO. No. Leave him alone. He wants an excuse to change the subject. Start a fight and you'll forget what you were arguing about.

JOHNNY. Listen! (*As if with great restraint*) You can have the money. There's exactly seven hundred and fifty pounds. You can take it all. I doubt if Dave would touch it.

CALICO. Where is it?

JOHNNY (*pointing to the door up* R) It's in there. It's hidden under a floorboard. Do you want it just now?

MIKE (*belligerently*) Yes, I do.

CALICO. Why not?

JOHNNY. Why not? (*He crosses down* L) I'll tell you why not, my pet. Because we're still due a visit from the gentlemen investigating the murder that took place as recently as two nights ago. Because they're likely to come here. And when they come they may have a search warrant. Where it is now they'll never find it. Do you still want it?

(MIKE *moves and sits* L *of the table*)

CALICO (*to Mike*) For Pete's sake, don't let him out-talk you every time. What use is it under the bedroom floor? We can't sail to China on a frozen asset, can we?

JOHNNY. Who the hell's going to China?

CALICO. We are. (*She crosses to* C) The police haven't been yet, Mike. Perhaps you're right. Perhaps the old man is dead after all. It's crazy, but—as Johnny says—it could be. We can fly to Paris, Rome. Stay here and you're sitting on a time bomb. One day it'll go up, and so will we. (*She moves up* R) Let's get out of here.

MIKE. What do you think, Johnny?

JOHNNY. I've told you what I think.

CALICO (*crossing to* R *of Mike*) Let's go, I tell you. You've done a lot of talking, Mike. Let's have some action.

JOHNNY (*cuttingly*) We've had some action, haven't we?

CALICO. Let's have some more. We're not getting any younger. How long do you expect me to go on waiting for you? Till the stars tumble out of the sky? I'm not the waiting kind. Go now, and I'll go with you. Willingly. I'm going, anyway. With you— or alone. Which way do you want it?

MIKE. Could we get out of the country?

CALICO. Why not?

Johnny. If you take the money, you'll have to get out of these rooms. You can't stay here with it.

Calico. All right, I'm going.

Mike. No.

(*The sound of the violin is heard off*)

Calico (*moving down* r) Oh, yes, I am.

Mike (*rising*) We'll both go. (*To Johnny*) Where's the money?

(Johnny *shrugs, hesitates, then crosses and exits up* r)

Calico (*moving to Mike; smiling*) Thank you, Mike. (*She reaches up and kisses him*)

(Mike *is bewildered and dull*)

I'll make up for everything you've done for me. Don't look like that, Mike. We'll be together.

Mike. I wonder if I know what I'm doing.

Calico. Of course you do. Johnny's furious. He likes his own way, that's all. (*She crosses to the fireplace*) He thinks he's the smart one. He thinks he can twist you round his little finger. I could have died when you stood up to him. He had it coming.

Mike. No, Calico. (*He shakes his head*) Johnny has more brains in his little finger than I've got in my head.

Calico. He's no Einstein.

Mike. Perhaps we ought to—I don't know.

Calico (*freezing*) If you've changed your mind you'd better say so.

Mike (*beating the palm of his hand with a fist*) I don't know. I don't know. (*Impassioned*) To get you I broke into Mallaby's. I murdered old Joe Ryan.

(*The sound of the violin grows louder*)

Calico. You didn't mean to.

Mike (*moving up* r) But I did it. I did it. (*He shouts to Johnny*) Put a move on in there. (*He turns to Calico*) By God, if I can go so far for you I can go the rest of the way. We'll go. I don't know where to—I just don't know—but we'll go somewhere. (*He begins to pace the room, repeating the movement of fist against hand*)

(Calico *observes him quietly*)

(*He moves to the window*) There goes that damned old fiddle again. (*He gazes through the window a moment, down at the street, then opens the window and shouts*) Stop making that blasted noise! (*He closes the window*)

(*The violin ceases abruptly.*

Johnny *enters up* r. *He carries a brown paper parcel which he places on the table*)

JOHNNY. Take it. It's yours. (*He moves up* c)

(MIKE *and* CALICO *stare at the parcel for a moment*)

CALICO. Open it, Mike.

(MIKE *does not move*)

Go on, open it up.

JOHNNY. Yes, go on, Mike. You asked for it. What are you staring at?

MIKE (*subdued*) I only want my share.

JOHNNY. No, you don't. Pack your bags and take it with you.

MIKE. What do you say, Calico? (*He moves to the table*)

(CALICO *moves to the table*)

(*He touches the parcel, picks it up, then puts it down again on the table*)

Seven hundred and fifty pounds.

JOHNNY. Are you afraid of it?

MIKE. No.

JOHNNY (*crossing to the easy chair down* L *and sitting*) It's scalding his fingers. (*He picks up Calico's book from the chair and reads the title*) "*The Woman Who Dared.*" I didn't know you could read, Calico. (*He turns the pages*) This is good literature, Mike. Living with Calico will improve your mind.

(MRS FINNEGAN *enters down* R)

MRS FINNEGAN. There's a gentleman to see you.

(PATRICK RYAN *enters down* R *and crosses to* RC)

Which Mr Farrell did you want to see? There's two of 'em in. The little one's out.

JOHNNY. Patrick Ryan! I haven't seen you in years.

RYAN. Hello, Johnny.

JOHNNY (*rising*) Come in. One of these days Mrs Finnegan is going to break the door down knocking so hard.

(MRS FINNEGAN *sniffs rudely and exits down* R, *closing the door behind her*)

RYAN. Hello, Mike.

(MIKE *nods gloomily*)

JOHNNY. This is Calico, Mike's fiancée. You didn't think he was the marrying type, did you? It seems that he is. (*To Calico*) This is Patrick Ryan.

(RYAN *crosses to* c)

(*To Ryan*) Pat, I'm sorry about—about your father.

RYAN. Thanks, Johnny.

JOHNNY (*to Calico*) Pat's father was night watchman at the works.

CALICO. Oh!

JOHNNY. Sit down, Pat. Will you have a drink?

RYAN (*sitting in the easy chair* LC) No—no, thanks.

JOHN (*crossing down* R) We can soon get a couple of bottles.

RYAN. I never touch it when I'm on duty.

(*The others look sharply at Ryan*)

MIKE. On duty?

RYAN. Police.

MIKE. Are you in the police?

RYAN. Detective-sergeant.

(CALICO *sits above the table*)

MIKE. I didn't know.

RYAN. I was three years in Birmingham. After they promoted me they moved me here. That was six weeks ago.

JOHNNY (*crossing and sitting* L *of the table*) I didn't know. I've been away a long time.

RYAN. You were in London, weren't you?

JOHNNY. Yes. I didn't like London. Too big for a little fish, so I came back to swim in the old pond.

RYAN. I see.

MIKE (*after a pause*) I suppose you're on—on the case?

RYAN. Father was murdered in cold blood. He was a good man. You knew him—Mike—Johnny—you both knew him. You remember how he used to play with us when we were kids.

JOHNNY. He was all right.

RYAN. He was rough, and pretty ignorant, but he was kind and generous. We're looking for his murderers.

JOHNNY. Do you know anything yet?

RYAN. No. (*Never for a moment in this scene does he imply in the least that he might suspect them*) What sort of men could they be who murdered a man like he was? He never hurt anybody in his life.

MIKE (*moving up* C) Perhaps—they didn't mean to do it.

RYAN. They had a gun, didn't they?

MIKE (*moving to the fireplace*) Yes.

RYAN. He was seventy years old.

JOHNNY. They shouldn't have killed him.

RYAN. I think they had to.

CALICO. What do you mean?

RYAN. I think they were frightened.

CALICO. If they had a gun, why were they frightened of an old man?

RYAN. Perhaps he recognized them.

JOHNNY. You mean it was someone he knew?

RYAN. I think so. Don't you?

JOHNNY. I've no idea.

RYAN. Father wasn't alone. One of his old Army friends was with him, an old boy called Danny. He often sat up talking with father.

JOHNNY. It's a lonely job, I suppose.

RYAN. Yes. (*He pauses*) He's disappeared.

JOHNNY. Dave told us.

RYAN. I'm trying to find out where he is.

JOHNNY. You mean he was there when—when it happened, but you haven't seen him since?

RYAN. That's right.

CALICO. How could that be?

RYAN. I have a theory.

CALICO. You think he was frightened?

RYAN. What of?

CALICO. Well—that you'd think he was the murderer.

RYAN. No, I don't think so. There's only one conclusion I can draw. I think the murderers took him away.

MIKE. No.

RYAN (*to Mike*) Why not?

MIKE. Well—they—they couldn't.

RYAN. I think they might.

(MIKE *crosses to the easy chair down* L *and sits*)

JOHNNY. You think they kidnapped him?

RYAN. It's feasible, isn't it?

JOHNNY. I suppose it is.

RYAN. You see, we know he was there when the murder was committed. So he would be able to testify against them. If we could find him our case would be solved.

CALICO. If they'd go so far, why didn't they shoot him, too?

RYAN. Perhaps they did.

CALICO. But you said not.

RYAN. Perhaps they killed him later.

MIKE (*spontaneously*) No . . .

JOHNNY (*rising; quickly*) That's quite possible. (*He crosses to the fireplace*)

MIKE. Oh, yes.

JOHNNY. Are you sure you won't have a drink, Pat?

RYAN. I'm a conscientious policeman. I never touch it when I'm on duty.

CALICO (*pointedly*) Are we to take it you're on duty now?

RYAN. Until I hang my father's killers I'll always be on duty.

CALICO. You don't think we did it, do you?

RYAN (*very surprised*) No. (*After a pause*) But it was what we call an inside job. One or more of Mallaby's employees must have had a hand in it. So, of course, I have to interview everybody. (*He looks at Mike and Johnny*) Did you think I suspected you?

(MIKE *and* JOHNNY *smile and shrug in innocent reaction*)

Of course, you *could* have done it. Your brother Dave is in the office. Mike here is an employee.

JOHNNY. Now look here, Pat . . .

RYAN. But a lot of other people had the same opportunity. Mallaby's is a big business.

CALICO. Then you've got to talk to a lot of people.

RYAN. That's true.

CALICO. It'll take a long time.

RYAN. It may. (*He rises*) Unless, of course, we find the old man. That would automatically solve the problem.

JOHNNY. You'd have an identification parade and he'd do the work for you.

RYAN (*moving up* R *of the table*) Something like that.

CALICO. It's the first time I was under suspicion of murder. I don't think I like it.

RYAN. Why are *you* under suspicion?

CALICO. Isn't everybody?

RYAN. Scarcely. In fact, nobody is—directly.

(MIKE *rises*)

JOHNNY (*crossing to* L *of the table*) You're very welcome here, Pat, any time. But you must admit it's rather an unhappy occasion. Would you like to ask us any questions?

CALICO (*rising and crossing to the door down* R) If you don't want me, I'll go to my room. Maybe I'm cramping your style. (*She opens the door*)

RYAN. If you wish, but there's no need. (*He half-sits on the edge of the table, moving the parcel to make room for himself*)

(*The others gasp as* RYAN *touches the parcel.* CALICO *hesitates at the door, then closes it and remains in the room*)

JOHNNY. If we can help at all . . .

RYAN. I suppose you don't know anything, do you?

(JOHNNY *shakes his head*)

Can you suggest anything? Have you heard any loose talk?

JOHNNY. Nothing.

MIKE. They wouldn't be likely to talk, would they?

RYAN. Sometimes. One of them might have threatened to burgle the cash desk six months ago, or a year ago, when he didn't seriously intend to do anything of the kind.

JOHNNY. I see what you mean.

MIKE (*anxiously*) You mean me, don't you?

JOHNNY. Why you?

MIKE. I'm always making threats like that.

CALICO. Mike, what on earth are you talking about?

MIKE (*crossing to* C) Well, you know how I am. I've got a big mouth. I've got a chip on my shoulder. (*To Johnny*) You always say I've got a grievance against the world.

JOHNNY. You have. But you never talked of burgling Mallaby's.

MIKE. Perhaps I did. I might have. If I see a Rolls Royce I'm sort of jealous of the man who's driving it. I say, if I'd been born in the same bed he was, it would be mine. I've a feeling to take it.

JOHNNY (*alarmed*) But you never do.

MIKE (*moving up* LC) No. I just want to. I never do.

CALICO. You silly fool, talking like that in front of Mr Ryan. He'll begin to suspect you.

JOHNNY (*to Ryan*) Were you referring to Mike?

RYAN (*quietly surprised*) No.

(CALICO *crosses down* L)

JOHNNY. You know Mike. He always does talk out of the back of his neck. It doesn't mean anything.

RYAN (*at a tangent*) There's nothing you can tell me, then?

JOHNNY. Nothing at all. (*He sits* L *of the table*) Are there any more questions you want to ask? (*He indicates Mike and Calico*) They were going to the *Odeon*.

RYAN (*rising and moving down* RC) I won't keep you any longer. I'm sorry you can't tell me anything. (*He indicates the parcel*) I'm passing the Post Office. Can I post this for you?

JOHNNY. No. No, thanks.

RYAN. It wouldn't be any trouble.

CALICO (*moving up* C) It's mine. They're—they're a few things I bought in town.

RYAN (*moving to the table and causually examining the parcel*) It's very badly tied. Shop assistants are so careless these days.

MIKE. Why?

RYAN. This is a slip knot. If I give it a sharp pull the whole parcel will fall apart.

CALICO (*moving quickly above the table*) No!

RYAN (*turning from the parcel*) Sorry.

CALICO. Not at all. I just didn't want all my underclothes littering the table.

RYAN. It's been nice to see you again, Johnny, after all these years. (*To Calico*) We're the same age. Mike could always— (*he moves to the door down* R) lick us with one hand tied behind his back.

CALICO. But Johnny was the one with the brains.

(RYAN *turns and smiles quizzically*)

RYAN. No. Johnny wasn't the one with the brains. I was. In

the long run I always came out on top. (*He opens the door*) Do you mind if I call in to see you again—just for a chat? I know you're as keen as I am to get this business sorted out.

JOHNNY. Of course. Any time.

RYAN. So long.

(RYAN *exits down* R, *closing the door behind him*)

MIKE. Johnny . . .

(JOHNNY *rises, and signals to Mike not to speak, indicating that Ryan may be listening at the door*)

JOHNNY (*in case Ryan can hear*) I haven't seen Pat for six or seven years. He doesn't look a day older.

(*There is a silence, during which* JOHNNY *crosses down* R *and* MIKE *takes a glass from the table and fills it with water from the sink*)

CALICO (*to Mike*) You were a prize idiot, weren't you?

(MIKE *drinks and puts the glass on the table*)

JOHNNY. Shut up! (*He moves to the window*) You're right. He raises stupidity to the level of genius, but it's no use talking about it. We've got to be careful. Rowing at each other won't help. (*He moves up* C. *To Mike*) In future let the secrets of your soul remain unspoken. That's all. (*He moves up* L *of the table. To Calico*) Let's hear no more about it. (*He picks up the parcel. To Mike*) Do you want it? (*He pauses. To Calico*) What do you say?

(CALICO *ignores Johnny.*
JOHNNY *exits with the parcel up* R)

MIKE. Did you hear what Ryan said?

CALICO (*sitting above the table*) Certainly I heard what he said.

MIKE. In the long run he always comes out on top.

CALICO. Yes.

MIKE. He knows we did it.

CALICO. I don't think so. But my heart was in my mouth when he got hold of the parcel.

MIKE (*crossing and sitting in the easy chair down* L) If he'd pulled at it we'd be in jail.

CALICO. Well, he didn't pull at it.

MIKE. Do you think he knows?

CALICO. I don't know. He hasn't any evidence or he'd have done something about it.

(JOHNNY *enters up* R, *goes to the window and looks down at the street*)

(*To Johnny*) Has he gone?

JOHNNY. Yes.

CALICO. Does he know?

JOHNNY. Ryan is clever. I don't know. I think he suspects us, but I don't know. He was always shrewd. (*He moves down* C) If he suspected us, but had no proof, that's the way he would act.

MIKE. Then he does suspect us.

JOHNNY. If he didn't—if such a thought never entered his head—that's the way he would act, too. (*He moves up* C) So we're in the dark.

MIKE. What can we do?

CALICO. We can do two things. Sit down and wait until he finds his evidence. Or get out of here fast.

JOHNNY. If you run away, he'll know why you're running away. If you spend more money than usual he'll have means of knowing. All we can do is sit and wait. If the bomb goes off, we've had it. If it doesn't, we're all right. Without the old man they can't do a thing.

MIKE. They'll find him all right.

CALICO. You're a little optimist. You said he was dead.

MIKE. That's our only hope.

JOHNNY. And—you know—I think he *is* dead. (*He moves up* RC) It sounds crazy, but I think he is. Ryan says he may be been kidnapped. We know better. He was there when we left. There's no other explanation. (*He moves up* C) He's got to be dead, or dying, or something like that.

CALICO. If he's dying he may not die. He may get better. Maybe we should move after all.

MIKE. But where?

JOHNNY (*moving to the window*) I think he's dead. I think the shock killed him.

CALICO. Mike ought to give exhibitions. He did a great job. He killed two men with one bullet.

MIKE (*rising and moving to the fireplace; explosively*) Why did you give me the gun?

(CALICO *takes a cigarette from the packet on the table, and lights it*)

JOHNNY (*quietly*) You gave him the gun. I wondered. Why did you?

MIKE. She got it from a soldier.

CALICO. I didn't expect him to use it.

JOHNNY. But he did. All right, I'm not going to argue about it. You gave it to him and he used it. Let's not argue. (*He moves down* C) The more I think about it the more I realize we have to keep together. Whether we like it or not that's how it is. We're stuck with each other. (*He sits* L *of the table*) We've got to keep our heads. We don't know where we are. We're sitting on a box in a dark room. There may be dynamite in the box, or they may not. We can't tell. Either way we've got to be smart. If we quarrel amongst ourselves we may as well sign a confession and save ourselves a lot of worry. Is that clear?

D

(The sound of the violin is heard off)

CALICO. It's clear enough.

JOHNNY. Then that's all right. I hope Dave isn't getting plastered. I think we ought to go and find out. *(To Mike)* Where will he be?

MIKE. *The Golden Fleece* is just round the corner.

JOHNNY *(rising and moving RC)* Let's go and look for him.

(There is a hasty knocking at the door down R)

CALICO *(rising; quickly)* Did you hide the money?

DAVE *(off)* Let me in.

(JOHNNY moves quickly to the door down R and opens it.
DAVE enters down R. He has a strange look of bewilderment and fear. The sound of the violin becomes louder)

JOHNNY. What's the matter with you? It isn't locked.

(DAVE crosses to C)

MIKE. He's drunk.

DAVE. I had one glass. Only one glass.

CALICO. Sit down, Dave.

(DAVE sits in the easy chair LC)

JOHNNY. You look as if you've seen a ghost.

DAVE. A ghost?

CALICO. You're ill. What happened to you?

DAVE. I saw the old man.

JOHNNY. Quiet! *(He closes the door and crosses to R of Dave)*

MIKE. How do you mean, you saw the old man?

DAVE. The old man at Mallaby's.

JOHNNY. You can't have seen him. Listen, the police have been here. He's missing. They don't know where he is.

DAVE. I do. I know. I just saw him.

MIKE. You're drunk.

DAVE. No. I tell you I saw him.

JOHNNY. Don't be a fool.

DAVE. Stop shouting at me. Go and look for yourself. He's still there. He's still playing.

JOHNNY. What on earth are you talking about?

DAVE. It's the old man, the one who saw us kill Joe Ryan. Believe me, I'm not drunk, I've just been walking the streets. I've been thinking. Walking and thinking. When I went out I passed the old fiddler. I gave him a penny. I see him nearly every day of my life. And then, when I came back, he was still there, higher up the street. And I looked at him, and . . .

JOHNNY. Well?

DAVE. It wasn't him.

JOHNNY. How do you mean, it wasn't him?
DAVE. It was the old man at Mallaby's.

(JOHNNY *moves up* R)

You don't believe me, do you? But it was. He wore the fiddler's clothes and he had his old fiddle. But it was the old man from Mallaby's.
JOHNNY (*to Mike*) Put him to bed.
DAVE (*rising and moving up* C) Do you think I'm mad?
JOHNNY. Have a sleep. You're worried. We're all worried, Dave. Lie down for half an hour. Rest.
DAVE (*laughing*) Just like that. All right, Johnny, but go and see for yourself. He's still playing. He's still playing.
MIKE (*rising and crossing down* R) I'll go, Dave, if you want me to.
DAVE. You'll see I'm right.

(MIKE *exits down* R. *The violin music ceases*)

(*To Johnny*) I was only six feet away from him. I couldn't be mistaken, Johnny.
JOHNNY. All right.
DAVE (*moving to the window*) He's still playing.
JOHNNY. Of course he is. Get a hold of yourself, Dave. It's just imagination. A complex. It's on your mind. The old man's face has got on your nerves. It's just a form of anxiety. Hell, I'm not a psychiatrist or I'd give you all the fancy words.
DAVE (*crossing down* R) No. It was him. You'll see. Wait until Mike comes back. He'll tell you.
CALICO. Johnny's right, Dave.
DAVE. Oh, no. It was the old man. You're staring at me as if I'm crazy. I saw him with my own eyes. (*He crosses to* LC) It could be a trick, couldn't it?
CALICO. How?
DAVE. Some trick the police are playing on us. Perhaps they're playing on our nerves. (*He sits* L *of the table*) Trying to wear us down.
JOHNNY (*winking at Calico*) Perhaps he's right. If he saw the old man, it must be the old man. We can't get away from fact.
DAVE. Thank God somebody believes me at last.
JOHNNY. It's upset you, hasn't it, Dave?
DAVE. Yes. (*Suspiciously*) Do you believe me?
JOHNNY. I've no choice in the matter. You're not a fool.
CALICO (*moving to Dave*) Lie down a little, Dave. Please.
DAVE. She thinks I'm crazy.
JOHNNY. No, she doesn't. But your nerves are on edge. You won't deny that, will you?
DAVE. I can't. It's true.
JOHNNY. Then do as Calico says.

CALICO. They sent you home from Mallaby's because you were ill. You shouldn't have gone out again.

DAVE (*rising*) All right.

(CALICO *leads* DAVE *up* R *and exits with him, and re-enters almost immediately*)

CALICO (*crossing to the table; quietly*) He's going off his rocker. Can you see Mike?

JOHNNY (*looking through the window*) He's coming back.

CALICO. What do you think?

JOHNNY. I don't like it.

CALICO. Do you think he's going queer?

JOHNNY. If he does, we're sunk. He'd collapse. He'd give the game away. He mustn't go back to Mallaby's. Another day and he'll break down. It's a chance we shall have to take.

CALICO. He's pretty childish, isn't he, for a grown man?

JOHNNY. But you didn't see Joe Ryan die, did you?

(MIKE *enters down* R)

MIKE. What do you make of Dave? He passes that beggar a couple of hundred times a year. How could he be so stupid?

CALICO. It—wasn't the—the other man, was it?

MIKE (*crossing and sitting in the easy chair* LC) Of course it wasn't.

JOHNNY. Did you say anything to him?

(*The sound of the violin is heard off.* CALICO *sits above the table*)

MIKE. No—why should I?

JOHNNY (*looking through the window*) He's coming this way. (*He turns to face the others*) I don't like it. It's—it's unnatural. It's like a ghost story. What's happening to us? (*He moves down* C) Tell me that—what's happening to us all? (*He moves to the window and looks out*)

They are all motionless. The sound of the violin grows louder and louder. CALICO *and* MIKE *exchange looks, then both look at* Johnny *at the window as—*

the CURTAIN *falls*

ACT III

SCENE I

SCENE—*The same. Morning. Three days later.*

When the CURTAIN *rises,* JOHNNY *is at the sink up* L, *shaving, looking at his reflection in a small wall mirror over the sink.* CALICO *is sprawling on the divan, facing forward, but turning to watch Johnny. She wears a little smile.*

JOHNNY (*turning*) What are you laughing at?

CALICO. I'm not laughing.

JOHNNY. Well, smiling, then.

CALICO. I think men look funny when they're shaving.

JOHNNY. How many have you seen?

CALICO. You'd be surprised.

JOHNNY. Oh, no, I wouldn't.

CALICO. You look cute. You know that, don't you? Your face looks like a peach wrapped in cotton wool.

JOHNNY. Don't be ridiculous. Where did Mike go?

CALICO. Out.

JOHNNY. Can't we be a little more specific?

CALICO. It's a wonderful big word. What does it mean?

JOHNNY. It means where did he go?

CALICO. Out.

(JOHNNY *glances at her*)

(*She smiles*) Did I ever tell you I'm in love with you?

JOHNNY (*startled*) You're . . . (*He recovers himself*) You're in great humour this morning, I must say. Unfortunately, I'm not.

CALICO. Not in love with me?

JOHNNY. Not in good humour. Or, for that matter, not in love with you. Why don't you go back to your room? I like a little privacy.

CALICO (*rising and moving to the window*) I hate being up there by myself. I don't sleep. It's a relief when daylight breaks. I mean it, you know.

JOHNNY (*casually*) Mean what? (*He finishes shaving*)

CALICO. I'm crazy about you.

JOHNNY (*wiping his face*) You're like the wind. You blow hot and cold. You change direction so fast you must be dizzy. Who will it be tomorrow—someone else?

CALICO. Maybe. Today it's you.

JOHNNY. Let's talk about something interesting. What's the weather like?

CALICO. This time it's real.

JOHNNY (*impatiently*) The weather. I'm talking about the weather.

CALICO (*moving up* LC) I was never in love with Mike. I liked him. I still do. But he isn't for me. He's too straight and honest.

JOHNNY. Honest? That sounds absurd—now—but it's true. He's perfectly honest, and he's guilty of burglary and—he still thinks you're wonderful, doesn't he?

CALICO. No. But he still wants me. So do you.

JOHNNY (*moving to Calico*) You've a pretty big opinion of yourself.

CALICO (*persisting*) Don't you?

JOHNNY. I dislike you intensely.

CALICO. I know you do. But you want me.

JOHNNY. Do I? (*He turns away*)

CALICO (*touching his arm*) Don't you?

JOHNNY (*turning; deliberately*) You—little . . . (*He seizes her in his arms and kisses her*)

(DAVE *enters down* R. CALICO *and* JOHNNY, *locked in a passionate embrace, do not see Dave*)

CALICO. Johnny.

JOHNNY. What is it about you, Calico . . . ? (*He sees Dave*) Dave! Dave!

(CALICO *turns and sees Dave.*
DAVE *exits silently down* R)

(*He crosses quickly to the door down* R, *opens it and calls*) Dave! (*He closes the door and turns*) That's fine. Now *he's* mad.

(CALICO *sits in the easy chair* LC)

If I've said it once I've said it fifty times—we've got to keep together. No rowing. No jealousy. My God!

CALICO. He isn't jealous.

JOHNNY. Of course he is.

CALICO. He has no right to be.

JOHNNY. I suppose you told him you loved him, too.

CALICO. No. He told me. I didn't encourage him.

JOHNNY. He isn't your type.

CALICO. No. You are.

JOHNNY. I think you're right. Who are you? They call you Calico. What are you? Where do you come from?

CALICO. That's quite a question.

JOHNNY. How did we get entangled with you, that's what I'd like to know. No, don't tell me. You don't know. (*He crosses to* C) You happened to meet Mike on the stairs. They say we're all puppets on a string and the Fates are juggling with us. What sort of Fate caused your string to get crossed with ours?

CALICO (*rising and moving close to him; very earnestly*) I don't know, Johnny.

JOHNNY (*quickly*) I think you came out of the slums . . .

CALICO (*also quickly*) I did.

JOHNNY. You're an outsider. You don't belong with us.

CALICO. No, I don't. I don't.

JOHNNY. But some mischievous pull at the strings brings you into our existence. Why? (*He puts his arms around her*)

CALICO. You tell me, Johnny. I don't know.

JOHNNY. Mike was as straight as a die. Dave, too. They hadn't a wrong thought in their simple heads before you came along.

CALICO. Kiss me, Johnny.

JOHNNY. How did it happen, Calico?

CALICO. Kiss me.

(*They embrace with the same great fervour as was previously displayed. Suddenly, but quietly, they separate. CALICO moves LC. Her lightness, her coarse sensuality, have evaporated. JOHNNY turns and faces down R., so that they have their backs to each other*)

JOHNNY. We shan't do this again. Do you hear me?

CALICO. Yes.

JOHNNY. I know I'm the born waster in this family, but I won't allow this to happen again. I—I imagine we were made for each other. Neither of us is on bowing terms with goodness and the things that make life civilized. We'd get on together.

CALICO. Wonderfully.

JOHNNY (*moving up R*) But we're not going to. Stay away from me.

CALICO (*turning*) Can you stay away from me?

(JOHNNY *turns and they look at each other.*

MRS FINNEGAN, *abrupt as ever, enters down R. She faces Johnny and then impudently, knocks on the inside panel of the door*)

MRS FINNEGAN. What about the rent?

JOHNNY. Rent? Oh! (*He takes out his wallet and hands some notes to Mrs Finnegan*)

MRS FINNEGAN. I haven't any change.

(CALICO *moves up* C)

JOHNNY. Later.

MRS FINNEGAN. I'll bring it when I come up to do the landing. (*She glances with disfavour at Calico*) Oh, I forgot to tell you. Somebody called to see your brother.

(CALICO *crosses and sits on the divan*)

JOHNNY. Yes?

MRS FINNEGAN. I said I'd seen him go out and he said he'd call back.

JOHNNY (*moving* C) Was it Dave he asked for?

MRS FINNEGAN. No, the big one.

JOHNNY. Mike?

MRS FINNEGAN. Yes. He told me his name, but I forget it.

JOHNNY (*crossing down* L) He'll come back, I suppose.

MRS FINNEGAN. He was an old man.

JOHNNY. Who was he?

MRS FINNEGAN. Can't remember his name. He had a scar over his left eye. I'll bring the change when I do the landing.

(MRS FINNEGAN *exits down* R)

CALICO (*rising; alarmed*) Johnny!

JOHNNY. Hush!

CALICO (*crossing above the table to* LC) Was it . . . ?

JOHNNY. Quiet!

(MRS FINNEGAN *enters down* R)

MRS FINNEGAN. I remember what he said. He said: "Tell him Danny called to see him".

CALICO. Danny!

MRS FINNEGAN. That's what he said. I'll bring the change when I come up to do the landing.

(MRS FINNEGAN *exits down* R)

CALICO (*moving down* LC) Did the old man at Mallaby's have a scar over his left eye?

JOHNNY. Yes.

CALICO. The detective said his name was Danny.

JOHNNY. Yes.

CALICO. Then . . .

JOHNNY (*sitting in the easy chair down* L) Don't talk. It's absurd. It doesn't make sense. What does it add up to?

CALICO. Blackmail.

JOHNNY. What?

CALICO. It could be blackmail. He saw everything that happened. He didn't wait to see the police. Now he wants to blackmail you.

JOHNNY. He was an old pal of Joe Ryan. They were in the Army together at the Battle of Hastings. He wouldn't do a thing like that.

CALICO (*sitting in the easy chair* LC) He might. We'll soon know. He's coming back.

JOHNNY. I wonder.

CALICO. The old girl said so.

JOHNNY. Nothing happens that you might expect to happen. Logic and reason have no contact with us. The whole thing's complicated. If it's obvious we can assume it doesn't exist. If we see a thing we can be sure it isn't there.

CALICO. But we know that he's alive.

JOHNNY. Not necessarily.

CALICO. What do you mean?

JOHNNY (*rising and crossing to* c) Suppose the police found him dead. They think we're responsible, but they have no proof. What can they do? (*He moves up* c) They put clever boy Ryan on the job. He's as shrewd as they make 'em. He reads psychology. He knows the three Farrell boys inside out. He knows we're unstable. One minute we're in the dumps, and a minute later we go floating up into the stars. What does he do? (*He moves to the window*) I'll tell you. He starts a war of nerves.

CALICO. He couldn't *invent* the old man. However shrewd he is he couldn't bring him back from his coffin.

JOHNNY. No. But he could duplicate him.

CALICO. Say that again.

JOHNNY (*moving* c) Mrs Finnegan saw an old man with a scar. The descriptions tally, that's all.

CALICO. But Dave saw him, too.

JOHNNY. Dave was jumpy. He could be deceived easily enough. (*He crosses to the fireplace*) Any actor could make up—confuse him. Besides, Mike went out and said it was the old fiddler.

CALICO. So what?

JOHNNY. So we're as much in the dark as ever.

(DAVE *enters down* R)

DAVE. Have you finished with the big love scene?

JOHNNY (*emphatically*) Entirely.

DAVE. Who will be next? Ryan's a bachelor . . .

(JOHNNY *sits in the easy chair down* L)

CALICO. That's a rotten thing to say.

DAVE (*he laughs*) That'd be funny, wouldn't it? Full circle. (*He moves up* RC) "This is where we came in." (*Soberly*) I called to see Mr D'Arcy at the office this morning.

JOHNNY. Yes.

DAVE. I said I wanted to leave.

JOHNNY. Did he object?

DAVE. No. He said I wasn't under suspicion. I didn't have to feel unhappy about it. But if I wanted to leave it was all right.

JOHNNY. Did they look suspicious?

DAVE. Ryan was there.

JOHNNY. Oh!

CALICO. Did he talk to you?

DAVE. Yes. (*He sits above the table*) He said he was sorry I felt unhappy. He said I was the last man in the world who would kill his father. He said it was absurd of me to feel that he thought otherwise.

CALICO. Did he sound sincere?

DAVE (*quoting Johnny*) Entirely.

CALICO (*to Johnny*) But *was* he sincere?

(JOHNNY *rises and crosses to* L *of the table*)

DAVE. I collected my wages and they gave me my insurance card. Mr D'Arcy shook hands with me. One of the directors said I could go back when the murderers had been found. (*He laughs*) That was wonderful, wasn't it?

JOHNNY. Couldn't you tell whether they were sincere or not?

DAVE. No. Ryan walked with me out of the office. He said he could give me a lift into town if I wanted him to. He told me I was pale. The commissionaire opened his car door. I got in.

JOHNNY. Well?

DAVE (*expressionless*) The commissionaire was an old man—he had a scar over his left eye.

(JOHNNY *crosses to the fireplace*)

CALICO. It's crazy.

DAVE (*still expressionless*) Ryan dropped me in town. I said I would walk the rest. I left him at the corner of Talbot Street.

(JOHNNY *crosses above the table to* R *of it*)

There was a big Daimler drawn up at the kerb. Chauffeur-driven. The man in the back gave the chauffeur a parcel and he went into the bank with it. The man wore a top hat, morning cut-away coat and a fancy tie. He had a monocle in one eye.

JOHNNY. Go on.

DAVE (*looking askance at Johnny*) That was the old man, too.

CALICO. Crazy!

DAVE (*beginning to cry*) He had a scar over his left eye. It was the old man. Either it's a trick or else I'm going mad. Which is it, Johnny?

JOHNNY. You're not going mad.

DAVE (*crying*) I soon will. I can't go on like this.

(CALICO *rises, moves to* L *of Dave and puts her arm about his shoulders*)

CALICO. You're as sane as anybody in the world, Dave.

DAVE. Am I?

JOHNNY. Of course you are. It must have been a trick. Ryan dropped you there deliberately so that you'd see the man in the back of the car. At first you had a right to be worried, but not now. (*He crosses down* R) Believe me, Dave. It isn't the old man.

DAVE. Then who is it?

JOHNNY. Somebody dressed up by Ryan. A dummy. He's trying to get you down. He'll go on doing it. Try to see things as they are. Ryan hasn't a clue. He thinks it's us, but he isn't sure. He hasn't a shred of proof. (*He has a new idea*) He may be playing this game on a dozen people from Mallaby's. (*He moves c. Enthusiastically*) He may be working on everybody. If somebody cracks under the strain he finds his man. That's it. By heaven, I believe that's it.

(DAVE *rises, crosses to the sideboard, takes out a bottle of brandy and a glass and pours himself a drink*)

DAVE. How much money did we get?

CALICO. Seven hundred and fifty pounds. When it all blows over we'll be all right.

DAVE. I wouldn't go through this for seven hundred and fifty millions.

CALICO. You'd be in jail. Remember that. Now they don't know your accounts were wrong.

DAVE. Johnny, we've got to destroy the money.

JOHNNY. Have we?

DAVE. They've got a record of the numbers. If we spend it they could trace it to us.

JOHNNY (*crossing and sitting in the easy chair* LC) I know.

CALICO. You can't destroy it.

DAVE. We've got to.

JOHNNY (*quietly*) I already have.

CALICO. What!

JOHNNY. I burned it last night.

CALICO. Oh, no! Oh, no!

(JOHNNY *points towards the fireplace*. CALICO *crosses to the fireplace, kneels, picks up the poker and runs it through the ashes*)

JOHNNY (*ironically*) Do you still love me?

CALICO (*rising; with a laugh*) God, but it's a yell. It's delicious. All those plans, all those dreams, all that effort. Burglary. Murder. Everything but the kitchen sink. No, even that. For this. (*She throws the poker into the hearth*) Ashes to ashes. Don't you think it's funny, Dave?

DAVE. Very funny.

(CALICO *roars with laughter*)

JOHNNY. Are we still made for each other, Calico?

CALICO (*crossing to* R) If the hangman calls. I'll be in my room.
    (CALICO *exits down* R)

JOHNNY. It had to be destroyed.

DAVE. Yes.

JOHNNY. It really is the final touch, isn't it? It wraps things up beautifully. It's all been so futile.

DAVE. Do you love her?

JOHNNY. I don't know.

DAVE. I told you she was evil, didn't I? Do you remember?

JOHNNY. I remember.

DAVE. There's—something—*corroding* about her. She brings restlessness, dissatisfaction—a sort of wildness. Look how she's changed us all.

JOHNNY. It's convenient to blame her. But she only brought out something we'd kept under lock and key.

DAVE (*moving* c) No. She put it there. We didn't go to the crusades, or slay dragons or climb the highest mountain to get Calico. We cold-bloodedly murdered a man who was worth all three of us put together.

JOHNNY. It's no use blaming her.

DAVE. Now *you're* defending her.

JOHNNY (*crossing to the fireplace*) I'm trying to be fair.

DAVE. She's got into your blood. The same way she got in ours. I told you, she's evil. Evil.

(DAVE *exits up* R. JOHNNY *strolls thoughtfully about the room. He looks out of the window, then crosses to the sideboard and pours a drink for himself, holding the glass up to the light and examining it expertly. He glances around him. His attention falls on the gramophone up* R. *He moves to it, raises the lid and starts a record. The tune is of a violin playing "If I Should Fall In Love Again".* JOHNNY *stares at the gramophone for a moment, then puts his glass on the table.*

DAVE *enters up* R. JOHNNY *moves to the gramophone and switches it off*)

JOHNNY. Where did that record come from?

DAVE. You put it on, didn't you?

JOHNNY. It was on the gramophone.

DAVE. It doesn't belong to us.

(MRS FINNEGAN *enters down* R)

MRS FINNEGAN (*crossing to the table*) Here's your change. (*She puts some coins on the table*)

JOHNNY (*taking the record from the gramophone*) Mrs Finnegan, has anyone been in this room while we've been out?

MRS FINNEGAN. How do I know?

JOHNNY. Have you given anyone the key?

MRS FINNEGAN. I haven't come here to be insulted.

JOHNNY (*moving to* R *of Mrs Finnegan*) Do you know anything about this gramophone record?

MRS FINNEGAN (*looking at the record*) I've never seen it before. What's wrong with it.

JOHNNY. It isn't ours.

MRS FINNEGAN. I'm sure I don't know anything about it. It isn't mine. And I'm not in the habit of letting strangers into my lodgers' rooms, I'd like you to know.

Johnny. I'm sorry if I offended you.

Mrs Finnegan. I have my ethics.

Johnny. Yes. I—I'm sorry. May I offer you a drink?

Mrs Finnegan (*crossing to the door down* r) Never touch the stuff when I'm on duty.

Johnny. On duty?

Mrs Finnegan. Cleaning. I'm doing the landing.

Johnny. You said—on duty.

Mrs Finnegan. It was my little joke. Drink goes smack to my head. I'd look pretty soft tumbling down three flights of stairs. Well, I can't stand here all day.

(Mrs Finnegan *exits down* r)

Dave (*moving to the window*) That was a funny thing for her to say. Isn't it what Ryan said?

Johnny. It's just a coincidence.

Dave. We're having a lot of coincidences, aren't we?

Johnny (*moving up* c) Don't expect me to explain this.

Dave. I don't.

(Mike *enters down* r)

Johnny. Mike, do you know anything about this record?

Mike (*excitedly*) Never mind about that. Do you know where the old man is—the old man who was with Joe Ryan?

(Johnny *replaces the record on gramophone*)

I just saw him.

Johnny (*crossing to the fireplace; unperturbed*) You saw someone else. The police have dressed somebody up—perhaps an out-of-work actor—it isn't the same man.

Mike (*moving below the table*) You're mistaken, Johnny. I've seen him.

Johnny (*casually*) Yes, I know. They look the same. It's a trap. Next time you see him, don't hurry away. Talk to him. (*He sits in the easy chair down* l) You'll find he's a fake.

Mike (*simply*) I did talk to him.

(Johnny, *startled, rises.*
    Calico *enters down* r)

Calico. I thought I heard Mike come in.

Johnny. Shut up. (*To Mike*) You spoke to him?

Mike (*moving down* lc) Yes. It's him all right. Listen. (*He sits in the easy chair* lc)

(Calico *moves* c)

I was in Sloan's Saloon playing billiards with Henry Gale. Then I came out.

(DAVE *moves up* L *of the table*)

That's in Fenton Street. Next door there's a café. They have a few tables outside. That's where he was. He was sitting at a table with a cup of coffee. He looked at me and, at first, I was going to get out of his sight. Then I thought, no, we'll put an end to this.

DAVE. What did you do?

MIKE. Well, I went straight up to him and sat down.

JOHNNY (*alarmed*) No! You didn't!

MIKE. I did.

CALICO. Why shouldn't he?

JOHNNY. You damned numskull. (*He paces up and down* L.) The police were watching you. They were waiting to see if you recognized him. Ah, well, go on. What did he say?

MIKE. I'm no fool. I sat down. I didn't even look at him. I ordered a cup of coffee.

CALICO. Go on. Go on.

(JOHNNY *sits in the easy chair down* L)

MIKE (*proud of his technique*) I didn't look at the old man but I spoke to him. I said, "What's your game?" He sort of smiled. Then he said, "It's nice out here in the sun, isn't it?"

CALICO. That's a damn thing to say.

MIKE. I said again, "What's your game?" And he said, "What do you mean?" Then, what do you think happened?

DAVE. Go on—tell us.

MIKE. I heard a car drawing up at the kerb. It was an ambulance. A girl gets out—a smart girl. She was a nurse. She comes straight up to our table and goes to the old man. "Come along, Danny", she says. "We wondered where you were", she says. "Doctor Seed wants to see you," she says.

JOHNNY. An ambulance and a nurse.

MIKE. Then a man comes up from the ambulance. He's a big man, as big as me, all dressed in white. The old man went quietly, but this big fellow got a powerful grip on his arm and bent it behind him.

CALICO. He's insane.

MIKE. Yes. The ambulance came from an asylum.

DAVE. How do you know?

MIKE. The girl who served me the coffee said so.

(JOHNNY *rises*)

CALICO (*to Johnny*) Is that good or bad?

JOHNNY. It's like everything else. Incredible.

MIKE. I'm speaking the truth.

JOHNNY. I'm sure you are. But it isn't sense. (*He crosses and sits on the down right corner of the table*) I don't believe he's insane. I don't believe he's alive. And I don't believe he's dead. I don't believe anything.

DAVE. Did he ever exist?

MIKE. We know he did.

DAVE (*crossing to the fireplace*) Do we? Or is it a nightmare? I can't even think straight any more. (*He looks at Calico*) And it's all her fault. If we'd never set eyes on you we wouldn't be in this mess.

CALICO. I didn't ask you to rob Mallaby's in the first place.

MIKE. You're right. (*To Dave*) It was you. You wanted to take Calico away from me. (*Surprisingly*) You cast covetous eyes on your own brother's girl.

DAVE. She never was your girl. She was everybody's girl. Anybody's.

(MIKE *rises and moves angrily to Dave*)

Go on. Knock me down. Kill me. I wouldn't be the first notch on your gun.

(MIKE *grabs Dave*)

JOHNNY. Leave him alone.

MIKE. Why should I? Because he's small and useless, why do I have to let him say such things?

DAVE. Because they're true. (*He crosses above the table*) Ask Johnny. He knows. If you think she wants you you're wrong in the head. She's fooled us all. She's driven us all mad.

JOHNNY. Will you shut up?

DAVE (*moving down* R; *to Mike*) When I came in Johnny was kissing her. Ask him to explain that. Ask her.

(JOHNNY *rises and moves up* R)

MIKE (*to Calico*) Is that true? Did he touch you?

CALICO (*moving and sitting on the right arm of the easy chair* LC) Don't look at me like that. It was nothing.

DAVE (*laughing*) It was a platonic kiss. No passion. Just brotherly and sisterly affection.

(MIKE *moves slowly towards Johnny, then suddenly rushes at him, grabs him, struggles with him and forces him over the table*)

MIKE. You dirty, dirty rat.

CALICO (*rising*) Johnny, Mike, for crying out loud!

(MIKE *strikes Johnny.*

RYAN, *unseen by the others, enters down* R. *He knocks, as Mrs Finnegan did earlier, on the inside panel of the door. They all turn and stare at Ryan.* JOHNNY *gets up, tenderly holding his eye*)

DAVE. Ryan!

RYAN. It looks like an Irish holiday. Is it a private party, or can anyone join in?

MIKE. What do you want, Patrick Ryan?

RYAN (*crossing to* LC; *disarmingly*) You said I could drop in for a chat any time I felt like it. I hope I didn't choose the wrong moment. Isn't anyone going to offer me a drink? (*He sits in the easy chair* LC) I never indulge when I'm on duty, but I felt I might relax a little today. My search is practically at an end—I think.

RYAN *gazes forward with a bland expression on his face. The others watch him in silence as*—

the CURTAIN *falls*

SCENE 2

SCENE—*The same. Morning. Three days later.*

When the CURTAIN *rises, the bright sun is pouring in through the window.* DAVE *is sitting above the table. With a shaky hand he is pouring whisky from a bottle into a glass which rattles against the bottle. He drinks. His manner is nervous.* CALICO *enters down* R.

CALICO. Hello! Where is Johnny?

DAVE (*a dreadful female impersonation*) "Where is Johnny?" I can remember when it was—(*impersonation again*) "where's Mike?" (*He smiles cunningly*) He's packing his suitcase.

CALICO (*moving to* R *of the table*) Johnny?

DAVE. Yes. Johnny. I think he's very wise.

CALICO. Do you mean he's going away? (*She moves to the door up* R, *knocks on it and calls*) Are you there, Johnny?

(JOHNNY *enters up* R. *He is in his shirt-sleeves*)

JOHNNY. Oh, hello!

CALICO (*mystified*) Hello. Dave says you're packing.

JOHNNY. Yes. I'm leaving.

CALICO. Oh!

(DAVE *bangs the bottle on the table, rises and moves to the door down* R.)

DAVE. Do you mind if I go? I hate to be one too many.

(DAVE *exits down* R)

JOHNNY. I'm sorry, Calico, but I can't stay here any longer.

CALICO. Where are you going?

JOHNNY. London.

CALICO. The little fish is going to the big pond again.

JOHNNY. That's it.

CALICO. Why? Why are you going?

JOHNNY (*crossing to the sink and collecting his shaving things*) Because I must. Things are getting too complicated here for my liking. Now Mike's like a bear with a sore tail because Dave saw me kissing you. I don't say I blame him. It was a rotten thing to do.

CALICO. No!

JOHNNY. How would you describe it?

CALICO (*moving up* C) Is it wrong to do something that's inevitable?

JOHNNY. The irresistible force and the—something-or-other body? I can't say.

CALICO. Will Ryan let you leave?

JOHNNY. He can't stop me. (*He crosses to the door up* R) He hasn't arrested me yet.

(JOHNNY *exits up* R, *taking his shaving things with him*)

CALICO (*moving to the door up* R) When are you going?

JOHNNY (*off*) There's a train this afternoon.

CALICO. This is good-bye then?

(JOHNNY *enters up* R *and crosses to* C)

JOHNNY. Yes. Calico, why haven't you gone away? You didn't have to stay. You'd no need to sit on the box of dynamite.

CALICO. I've got my own private box of dynamite that I'm sitting on. They call it love.

JOHNNY (*crossing to the divan*) Oh, come now! (*He picks up his cardigan from the divan and folds it*)

CALICO. You don't believe me. Well, I don't believe it myself. Me, the hard-boiled egg. I could laugh. (*She sits* L *of the table*)

JOHNNY. Anyway, I advise you to go away.

CALICO. Alone?

JOHNNY. It's safer that way.

CALICO. Maybe I don't want to be safe. Johnny, take me with you.

JOHNNY (*softly*) No.

CALICO. Please.

JOHNNY. I can't. At least, I wouldn't. It would be futile.

CALICO. Do you believe I love you?

JOHNNY (*moving to* R *of the table*) At this moment, yes.

CALICO. For keeps.

JOHNNY. It's no use. I told you, you blow hot and cold. You change colour with the time of the year. You'd give me too many headaches.

CALICO. I'd keep you on your toes.

JOHNNY (*crossing to the easy chair* LC) I'd be suspicious of the milkman, the postman, the boy who delivered the groceries. No, thanks. (*He collects a book from the chair*)

CALICO. I know I've always been like that. But no more.

JOHNNY (*crossing to the door up* R; *coldly*) Have you no pride? I'm telling you I don't want you.

E

(JOHNNY *exits up* R)

CALICO (*rising and moving up* C) I've no pride where you're concerned. I don't give up easily. Remember I'm from a slum. A rabbit's got more breeding than I've got. I'm like you.

(JOHNNY *enters up* R)

JOHNNY. Is that how low I've sunk?
CALICO (*moving above the easy chair* LC) It's how high you've climbed. Up to my low level. We're two of a kind.
JOHNNY. That's true. But it's a mistake for birds of a feather to flock together, especially if they're birds of prey. Look around for someone else, Calico; someone with ideals to lift you out of the gutter.
CALICO. I like it in the gutter. I belong there.
JOHNNY (*crossing to the sideboard*) Well, I don't. (*He takes a glass from the sideboard, moves to the table and pours a drink for himself*) Drink?

(CALICO *shakes her head*)

CALICO. You once asked me who I was—what I was. Well, my father was a wharf-rat. I never knew him. My mother only knew him for a couple of nights. (*She sits on the left arm of the easy chair* LC) When I was born she worked to keep me. She'd do anything to keep me. Anything. Do you understand? We lived in a filthy street on the wrong side of town. I only went to school sometimes because we kept moving. When she was in jail her friends took me in. That's my background.
JOHNNY. I'm sorry.
CALICO. You needn't be sorry. It made me tough. My hide's as thick as an elephant's. I'd no education, no manners, no charm. Just one thing. One day I found out I was attractive. I discovered my legs weren't just made to stand on. I discovered I had a talent. One talent, but that's all right—most people have no talent at all.
JOHNNY. That's me.
CALICO (*rising*) Just one talent, so I used it. Do you blame me? I was tough, and I got tougher. If you think I'm light-hearted you're not only mistaken, you're stupid. Do you think I like men? Do you think they attract me easily? Not on your life. The milkman, the postman, the delivery boy . . . That's really very funny. Shall I tell you why it's funny? (*She sits* L *of the table*) Because up till now I've steeled myself to put up with them, to let them kiss me and touch me. Because I could use them. They thought they were using me, but I knew what I was doing. At least—(*softening*) I think I did. (*Tearfully*) Now tell me your story.

(JOHNNY *crosses to the easy chair* LC *and sits on the right arm*)

JOHNNY (*kindly*) Don't you see, it's no use, Calico.

CALICO. The first time I really feel soft about a man—you tell me I'd be unfaithful. I was never unfaithful in my life. I never had anyone to be faithful to.

JOHNNY (*quietly*) There was Mike.

CALICO (*laughing, but not unkindly*) Poor old Mike. He was the first man who gave without wanting more than he gave. I treated him badly. He came on me too suddenly. (*She rises and crosses above Johnny to L of him*) If a dog gets used to being kicked he expects to be kicked. He probably bites the first hand that wants to stroke him. How was I to recognize the first decent man I saw? I just have talent—not genius. Johnny, you believe me, don't you?

JOHNNY. Yes.

CALICO. Every word?

JOHNNY. Every word.

CALICO. I'm glad you believe me. I'm glad. I'll go now. (*She crosses to c*) If you change your mind—if you want me—let me know.

JOHNNY (*rising and moving to L of Calico*) Of course I want you. You know damn well I want you.

CALICO. Johnny.

JOHNNY. Oh, what's the use? We're not in a meadow covered with daisies. We're not nice people, free and full of laughter and dreams. We're here, in this room. (*He moves to the window*) Dave's out there looking for an old man with a scar. Mike's out there—probably getting drunk. Ryan's out there—watching—like a cat playing with a mouse. Only he has three mice. Three blind, stupid, silly mice. There's no future, Calico. There's not even to-day. The sun's shining, but only because it shines on the Taj Mahal and a dung-heap both at the same time. What are you trying to do? Dream? (*He moves up c*) It's too late. It's too late.

CALICO. We could hide from them.

JOHNNY (*moving to the window*) For a day. Two days. Three.

CALICO. We'd make it seem like a lifetime.

JOHNNY. Would we? We don't deserve happiness. Have you forgotten Joe Ryan?

CALICO. Maybe he'd forgive us—if he knew.

JOHNNY. If he knew what?

CALICO. Maybe he knew what loneliness can do to you. Maybe he was born in a slum and hadn't the genius to climb out of it. Maybe he'd had *his* heart broken a thousand times.

JOHNNY. I wonder.

CALICO. A few hours of happiness. Even a vulture gets that much out of life.

JOHNNY. Even a vulture . . . Go and pack your things. I'll come for you in ten minutes' time. All right?

CALICO (*crossing to the door down R; radiant*) Yes. (*She opens the door*)

(MIKE *enters down* R)

MIKE (*subdued*) Hello.
CALICO (*very amiably*) Hello, Mike.

(CALICO *exits down* R)

MIKE (*moving up* C) Good morning, Johnny. (*He hangs his hat on the hooks*)

(JOHNNY *nods coolly*)

Johnny, I wanted to see you.
JOHNNY. Here I am.
MIKE (*crossing to the fireplace*) I've been thinking things over. About the other day. You and Calico.
JOHNNY. Mm!
MIKE. I'm sorry I went for you.
JOHNNY. Don't apologize. I don't blame you. Dave spoke the truth.
MIKE. Yes, I know.
JOHNNY. Well, then . . .
MIKE. I mean, it had to be. (*He turns the easy chair* LC *to face the fireplace and sits*) I'm no use to a girl like her. You're different.
JOHNNY. Am I?
MIKE. Yes. I'm just a big tramp. She's class. She could amount to something.
JOHNNY. Aren't you joking?
MIKE (*surprised*) No.
JOHNNY (*moving* C) You're not a tramp. You're the best of the lot of us. And you really mean it, don't you? That's true humility. No, Mike. Try not to be modest. In your heart you're a good man.
MIKE. I killed Joe Ryan.
JOHNNY. We all killed him.
MIKE. No. You didn't even know I had the gun.
JOHNNY (*crossing to the fireplace*) That doesn't make any difference to the police.
MIKE (*suddenly*) You have time to get away.
JOHNNY (*surprised*) Have I?
MIKE. You and—Calico.
JOHNNY (*crossing to* C) Perhaps we can all get away. I think we should try. I have a feeling they're closing in on us.
MIKE. Perhaps they'd be satisfied if they got me.
JOHNNY. Don't kid yourself.
MIKE. I don't want to go away.
JOHNNY. What are you, a twentieth-century martyr?
MIKE. I can't help it. It's how I feel. You go away while there's time, Johnny.
JOHNNY (*moving to the window*) All right, but you're going too.
MIKE. No, I'm not. Once, when we were kids, old Joe Ryan

practically saved my life. Do you remember? I'd climbed up a tree and I couldn't get down. He came up after me.

JOHNNY. You were only a kid. The tree wouldn't be as high as you thought it was.

MIKE. But he climbed up after me.

JOHNNY (*moving* c) Listen, Mike, you can't do anything for him now. God knows you didn't want to kill him. None of us wanted to. It was just something that happened.

MIKE. You can't wipe a murder off as easily as that.

JOHNNY. It wasn't murder.

MIKE. What do you call it then?

JOHNNY. You'd no malice. It wasn't planned. It was done on the spur of the moment.

MIKE. Manslaughter. That's a sweet word. (*He rises*) No, you go away, Johnny. I'm staying.

JOHNNY. Mike. I'll be honest with you. I am going away. With Calico. But you can't stay here. I couldn't let you.

MIKE (*sitting in the easy chair down* L) I'm staying. (*He takes a small book from his pocket and turns the pages*)

JOHNNY (*crossing to Mike*) Do me a favour, Mike. Do as I say.

MIKE. I've told you—no.

JOHNNY (*moving* c) At a time like this he reads a book.

MIKE. It's a remarkable book.

JOHNNY. What the hell is it?

MIKE (*looking up; simply*) It's a Bible, Johnny.

> (JOHNNY *shrugs helplessly.*
> DAVE *enters down* R)

JOHNNY (*to Dave*) I'm packing my things. I suggest you do the same.

DAVE. What about Mike?

JOHNNY. He's staying here.

DAVE. Where's Calico?

JOHNNY. She's going with me.

> (JOHNNY *exits up* R)

DAVE (*crossing to* LC; *quickly*) Calico and Johnny are going away together.

> (MIKE *is poring over the Bible*)

Ma always told us: "Johnny's the one one with the brains. You can always turn to him . . ." But he turned to us.

> (MIKE *rises, crosses and sits* L *of the table*)

He shared our rooms and he took your girl. Don't you care?

MIKE. No.

DAVE. I thought you'd got it bad. (*He moves to* L *of Mike*) What are you reading? (*He looks over Mike's shoulder*) What are *we* going to do?

MIKE (*looking up vaguely*) What's that, Dave?

DAVE (*moving above the table*) They are running away. What about us?

MIKE. I'm staying here.

DAVE (*moving to* R *of the table*) Aren't you frightened? Don't you think Ryan is close behind us?

MIKE. I do.

DAVE. Then—oughtn't we to go?

MIKE. You go, Dave. Have you any money?

DAVE. No.

(MIKE *takes five one-pound notes from his pocket and offers them to Dave*)

MIKE. It's all I have. I shan't need it.

DAVE. What about you?

MIKE. Take it.

DAVE. You're a good sort, Mike. Johnny steals your girl. I tried to. You know I tried to, don't you? Mike, she wouldn't have been any good to you. She's no good.

MIKE. I wouldn't have been any use to her. Take the money and go.

DAVE (*taking the notes*) Where will I go?

MIKE. As far as you can.

DAVE. I don't want to go alone.

MIKE. Talk to Johnny. He may have some ideas.

DAVE (*moving up* C) Yes. He's the one to turn to. Isn't it funny, Mike? We did so much for so little. Who'd have thought we should have become murderers? Do you know, Mike, we're the Farrell boys—killers. (*He moves up* LC) If we're arrested our photographs will be on the front pages of all the papers. People will look at us. They'll see you—big and simple and hasty, with a heart of gold—and they'll say, "He has a perverted mind". Me—I'm weak and frightened and I'm not worth a bag full of threepenny pieces, but I'm not what they'll imagine. And Johnny, smart-Alec Johnny with a little bit of education and a few big ideas and the gift of the gab—they'll say, "That's Johnny Farrell. He was the brains of the gang". Cold, ruthless, merciless——

(MIKE *rises and moves to the window up* RC)

—that's what we'll be. Wax figures in Madame Tussaud's. No one will know how frightened we were and that we only did it because a woman happened to meet a soldier who happened to giver her a gun. (*He laughs and crosses to the fireplace*) I say, it's rich, isn't it? Us—ruthless killers. (*Thoughtfully*) Johnny said, "She smiles, and the angels sing".

MIKE (*looking out of the window*) I think you're too late.

DAVE. Why?

MIKE. There's a police car parked across the street.

DAVE (*crossing to the window*) Is it Ryan?

MIKE. No. They've got a puncture.

DAVE. I've never seen a police car parked there before.

MIKE. They're jacking it up. One of them's unfastening the spare tyre.

DAVE. Or pretending to.

MIKE. Yes.

(JOHNNY *enters up* R. *He carries a small bag which he puts down near the door down* R)

JOHNNY. Oh, you've seen it, have you?

DAVE. What do you make of it?

JOHNNY. They wouldn't be there without a reason. It's a cul-de-sac.

MIKE. What's a cul-de-sac?

JOHNNY. It means a blind alley. There's no way out.

(*They pause, considering the symbolism of the phrase.* DAVE *crosses to the fireplace*)

No way out. (*To Mike*) Are you quite determined to stay here and read the Bible?

MIKE. Why not?

DAVE (*bitterly*) He hasn't got a girl to run away with, you know. For Mike and me there's nothing.

JOHNNY (*moving up* C) You want to go on living, don't you? (*He takes his coat from the hooks*)

DAVE. Go and leave us. Until you came we were all right. Go away and take the curse with you.

JOHNNY. That isn't fair, and you know it.

DAVE. Go away, Johnny, and take her with you. We'll wait here for whatever's coming.

JOHNNY. You're very brave all of a sudden. (*He moves down* C) For the last time, are you ready to go?

MIKE. No, Johnny.

JOHNNY (*hesitating awkwardly*) I shan't ask you again. What do you want me to do—go down on my knees.

MIKE (*crossing and sitting* L *of the table; smiling*) That wouldn't do you any harm, Johnny.

(*There is an uncomfortable silence*)

JOHNNY (*crossing to the door down* R) Oh, what the hell! (*He picks up his bag*)

(*There is a knock at the door down* R. JOHNNY *puts down his bag and opens the door.*
     RYAN *enters down* R)

RYAN. Hello! (*He crosses to* RC)

DAVE. I knew it was a trap.

RYAN (*surprised*) What do you mean, Dave?

DAVE. The car outside—punctured.

RYAN. Oh, that! (*He moves* C) He picked up a nail, I think. Even police cars have punctures, you know.

JOHNNY (*belligerently*) What do you want, Ryan?

RYAN. You never called me that before.

JOHNNY. I never called you what before?

RYAN. By my second name. You used to be more amiable. You've changed.

JOHNNY. I don't like your manner.

DAVE. If you've come to arrest us, why don't you say so?

JOHNNY. Come to the point.

RYAN. Why should I arrest you?

JOHNNY. Isn't that why you're here?

DAVE. What do you think we're made of? You sneak in here with a smile on your face and friendly words, and all the time you're laughing at us . . .

RYAN. I haven't laughed for a long time. What do you want me to arrest you for?

JOHNNY. You think we killed your father.

RYAN. Do I? Did you?

JOHNNY. No. Have you any proof that we did?

RYAN. How can I have if you didn't do it? (*He indicates Johnny's bag*) Were you going somewhere?

JOHNNY. What do you mean—*were* you going somewhere?

RYAN. All right, *are* you going somewhere?

JOHNNY. Yes. Calico and I. If you must know, we're going to be married.

RYAN. Calico—that's an odd name. But attractive. (*To Mike*) I thought she was your girl.

JOHNNY (*to Ryan*) Do you mind if we go? Have we your permission?

RYAN. I didn't know you required it.

JOHNNY. Oh! (*He picks up his bag and opens the door down* R) Then, good morning, Mr Ryan.

RYAN. I hope you will be very happy.

JOHNNY. We probably shall.

RYAN. There's just one thing before you go. You were fond of my father. I'm sure you'll be glad to hear that we finally trapped his murderers.

DAVE. Trapped them?

RYAN. Yes. What remains is purely a matter of routine.

(JOHNNY *closes the door*)

DAVE. Who—who is it?

RYAN (*taking a document from his pocket*) I have a confession here.

MIKE. You have a confession! (*He rises*)

RYAN. Yes. I won't bore you with the details. Roughly, though, it says: "I confess that I and my confederates on the night of May the fourth burglariously broke into the offices of Mallaby's, ironfounders, with the intention of stealing money. We were surprised by the night-watchman, Joseph Ryan, who challenged us, whereupon I—(*he looks for a moment and pauses*) produced a revolver and shot him dead". There are more words to it, of course, but that's what it amounts to.

DAVE (*to Johnny*) He has a confession.

JOHNNY. That's fine. (*He puts his coat and bag on the chair down* R) May I ask who signed it?

RYAN. Oh, it isn't signed.

JOHNNY. It isn't signed?

RYAN. But that's a mere formality.

DAVE. Why?

RYAN. I found the old man.

DAVE. I don't believe you.

RYAN. I generally speak the truth, Dave.

DAVE (*crossing to* C) Oh, no, you don't. You're an awful liar, Ryan. You think we killed him, don't you? But you can't prove it. You're trying to wear us down. All right, you're doing it. It isn't pleasant to be suspected of murder. It's horrible to know someone is working against you in the dark.

JOHNNY (*moving to* R *of Dave*) Dave!

DAVE (*backing away down* LC) He can't prove anything. Let's call his bluff. If the old man saw the murderers, and you know where the old man is, take us to him.

RYAN (*putting the document on the table*) You embarrass me, Dave.

DAVE. I'm sure I do. I can't stand it any longer, Ryan. Take us to him.

RYAN. Really!

JOHNNY (*acquiring confidence*) I think he's right.

DAVE. Of course I'm right. Bring him here, Ryan. If you have proof, arrest us.

RYAN. But I haven't even accused you.

JOHNNY. Do as he says, Ryan. You're no friend of ours. Bring the old man in here or get out. (*He crosses to* L)

RYAN. If that's how you feel. (*He crosses down* R)

JOHNNY. It is.

DAVE (*taunting; very assured, though near to tears*) Where is the old man, Ryan? Will it take long to bring him here? We'll wait, won't we, Johnny? Won't we, Mike?

RYAN (*quietly*) He's outside the door.

DAVE. He's—(*breathlessly*) outside the door?

RYAN. Yes.

DAVE. I—I don't—believe you.

RYAN (*moving to* R *of the table*) Are you sure you want him to see you? Is it necessary?

JOHNNY. I don't believe he's outside the door.

RYAN. Shall I bring him in?

JOHNNY (*doggedly*) Yes.

(RYAN *crosses to the door down* R *and opens it.*

THE OLD MAN, DANNY, *enters down* R *and crosses to* R *of the table.* DAVE, JOHNNY *and* MIKE *stand together* L *and stare at him.* RYAN *closes the door and crosses above the table to* LC)

RYAN. Well? Are these the men, Danny?

DANNY (*focussing his spectacles*) Yes. (*With assurance*) They're the ones.

RYAN (*calmly*) Are you sure?

DANNY. There's no doubt about it.

RYAN. You were there when they murdered Joseph Ryan?

DANNY. Yes, sir. They're the ones.

DAVE (*breaking down completely*) Johnny, Johnny—what are they doing to us?

JOHNNY. Get hold of yourself, Dave. (*He moves to the fireplace*)

(RYAN *moves to* DAVE, *helps him to the chair* L *of the table and puts the document in front of him*)

RYAN. I warn you that anything you say will be taken down and may be used in evidence.

JOHNNY. Don't sign it. For God's sake don't sign it.

MIKE (*calmly; as if he has made his peace with himself*) Why not? What difference does it make?

(CALICO *enters down* R)

CALICO. Johnny! (*She crosses to Johnny and embraces him*)

(DAVE *is hysterical and signs the document*)

DAVE. She gave him the gun.

(MIKE *crosses down* R)

(*He points to Calico*) She ruined us all. She's evil. She did it.

RYAN. All right.

(MIKE, *gazing steadily in front of him, exits down* R, *leaving the door open.* RYAN *helps* DAVE *to rise from the chair, and leads him* R. *As they go,* DAVE *points at Calico*)

DAVE. That's who did it. We didn't want to. We didn't mean to. It was Calico, I tell you. She gave him the gun. She gave Mike the gun. Calico. Calico. Calico.

(DAVE, *in wild tears, exits down* R, *assisted by* RYAN)

CALICO. Johnny!

JOHNNY. It's all over.

CALICO. I do love you, Johnny. This time it's real. You know that, don't you?

JOHNNY. Yes, I know.

CALICO. You do know it's true.

JOHNNY. I know. Yes, I know.

(RYAN *enters down* R. CALICO *crosses to the window and stands gazing out.* RYAN *begins to search the room, drawers, cupboards, etc. He picks up the gramophone record*)

RYAN. What did you do with the money? Burn it?

(DANNY *removes his spectacles.* JOHNNY, *on a sudden thought, crosses and faces Danny.* CALICO *and* RYAN *watch him.* JOHNNY, *very slowly, moves his hand in front of Danny's eyes. There is no reaction. Frantically, excitedly, he continues to wave his hand before Danny's eyes*)

JOHNNY (*quietly at first*) Oh, God! Ryan! He can't see. He can't see a thing. (*He turns to Ryan*) He's—he's blind, isn't he?

(RYAN *nods*)

Clever boy, Ryan. So we were right. You've been playing tricks with us. (*To Calico*) Isn't that beautiful? (*He moves up* C) He didn't see us—he didn't see us and he didn't recognize us, because he's blind, and Dave's down there, and Mike's down there, confessing. Now, isn't it beautiful? Isn't it really beautiful?

RYAN *crosses to* DANNY, *turns him round and guides him towards the door down* R. CALICO, *as if frozen into immobility, remains in the background.* JOHNNY *sinks into the easy chair* LC *and breaks into hysterical laughter. At first his laughter is short, spasmodic, and finally uproarious but wild with pain.* RYAN *and* DANNY *exit down* R *as—*

the CURTAIN *falls*

FURNITURE AND PROPERTY LIST

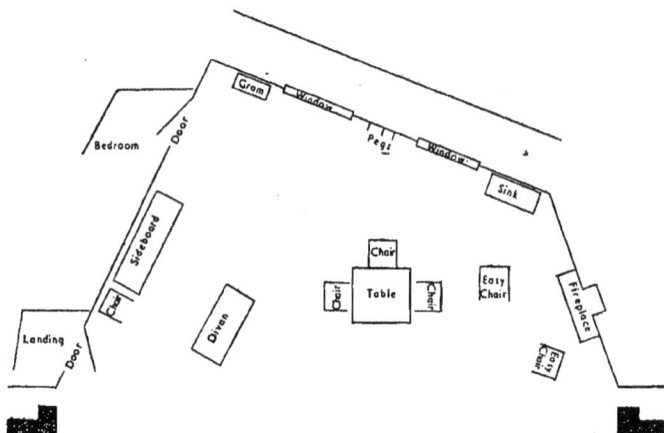

ACT I

SCENE I

On stage: Sideboard. *On it:* packet of cigarettes, bottle opener, tray
       In cupboard: 4 glasses
      Divan. *On it:* cushion
      2 easy chairs. *On them:* cushions
      Small chair (*down* R)
      Sink
      Over sink: wall mirror
      Towel rail: *On it:* tea-towel, face-towel
      Gramophone
      Table
      3 upright chairs
      Coat hooks on wall between windows
      Window curtains
      Carpet on floor
      Hearth rug
      Fire grate
      Fender
      Fire-irons
      Pictures on walls
      On mantelpiece: ornaments

Set: *On divan:* Johnny's overcoat, with newspaper in pocket, hat
      On table: tray, pot of tea, 2 cups, 2 saucers, 2 spoons, jug of milk,
         basin of sugar, 2 small plates, 2 small knives, plate with cheese,
         dish with butter, plate with bread and bread knife
Window curtains open
Fire lit
Light on

Off stage: 12 bottles of beer (DAVE and MIKE)

Personal: JOHNNY: note, packet of cigarettes, matches
         CALICO: scarf, wrist-watch

SCENE 2

Strike: Beer bottles
         Glasses
         Tea-things
Set: *On table:* racing journal
      On sideboard: 2 bottles beer, 4 glasses
Window curtains closed
Fire lit
Light on

ACT II

Strike: Beer bottles, glasses

Set: *On table:* packet of cigarettes, matches, ashtray
      On sideboard: bottle of beer, 2 glasses
      On easy chair down L: book
Window curtains open
Fire off
Light off

Off stage: Brown paper parcel (JOHNNY)

Personal: CALICO: watch

ACT III

SCENE 1

Strike: Beer bottles, glasses

Set: *At sink:* razor, towel, shaving brush, soap, mug of water
      In sideboard cupboard: bottle of brandy, glasses
      On gramophone: Record "If I Should Fall In Love Again"

Window curtains open
Fire off
Light off

Off stage: Coins (MRS FINNEGAN)

Personal: JOHNNY: wallet. *In it:* notes

SCENE 2

Strike: Brandy bottle, glasses

Set: *On table:* bottle of whisky, glass
      On divan: Johnny's cardigan
      On easy chair LC: book
      On sideboard: clean glasses
      On hooks up C: Johnny's coat
Window curtains open
Fire off
Light off

Off stage: Bag (JOHNNY)

Personal: MIKE: Bible, 5 £1 notes
          RYAN: document, fountain pen
          DANNY: spectacles

LIGHTING PLOT

Property fittings required: electric pendant c, fire (both practical)
strip outside door up R
strip outside door down R

Interior. A living-room. The same scene throughout

THE MAIN ACTING AREAS are at a table LC, at easy chairs LC and
down L, and at RC and C

ACT I, SCENE 1. Evening

THE APPARENT SOURCE OF LIGHT is an electric pendant c

To open: Blue outside windows up RC and up LC
Strips outside doors R
Pendant C, on
Fire, on

No cues

ACT I, SCENE 2. Evening

To open: Lighting as previous scene
No cues

ACT II. Morning

THE APPARENT SOURCES OF LIGHT are windows up RC and up LC

To open: Sunshine outside windows
Strips outside doors R
Pendant C, off
Fire, off

No cues

ACT III, SCENE 1. Morning

To open: Lighting as previous scene
No cues

ACT III, SCENE 2. Morning

To open: Lighting as previous scene
No cues

www.ingramcontent.com/pod-product-compliance
Lightning Source LLC
LaVergne TN
LVHW051758080426

835511LV00018B/3352